December 25, 1988

Judy,

Happy Quilting!

Love,
Marsha

HEARTS AND HANDS

The Influence of Women & Quilts on American Society

Hearts and Hands

The Influence of Women & Quilts on American Society

Concept by Pat Ferrero

Essay by Elaine Hedges

Photographic and quilt research, selection and captions
by Julie Silber and Pat Ferrero

THE QUILT DIGEST PRESS ▼ SAN FRANCISCO

Published in the United States of America by The Quilt Digest Press, San Francisco.

Editorial and production supervision by Michael M. Kile.
Book design by Patricia Koren and Laurie Smith, Kajun Graphics, San Francisco.
Cover design by Kajun Graphics, with Kristin Marx Meuser, San Francisco.
Editorial assistance provided by Harold Nadel, San Francisco.
Typographical composition in Simoncini Garamond by Rock & Jones, Oakland, California.
The majority of color photographs by Sharon Risedorph, with Lynn Kellner, San Francisco.
Calligraphy by John Prestianni, Berkeley, California.
Printed on 100 lb. Satin Kinfuji by Nissha Printing Company, Ltd., Kyoto, Japan.
Color separations by the printer.

Cover quilt: see page 71.

Cover photograph: a c. 1860–1870 ambrotype of two women with their sewing goods.
Collection of America Hurrah Antiques, New York City. Hand-colored by Sally Wetherby, Mill Valley, California.

Title page: detail of album quilt, by Eliza S. Howell, eastern United States, 1848, appliquéd cottons, with ink work.
Collection of Jo Graber, Yakima, Washington. Courtesy of the Yakima Valley Museum and Historical Association, Yakima.

First edition.
First printing.

Library of Congress Cataloging-in-Publication Data

Ferrero, Pat, 1942–
    Hearts and hands.

    Bibliography: p.
    Includes index.
    1. Women—United States—History—19th century.
2. Quilting—United States—History—19th century.
3. Quilts—United States—History—19th century—
Pictorial works. 4. United States—Industries—History—
19th century. 5. Material culture—United States—
History—19th century. 6. Material culture—United
States—History—19th century—Pictorial works.
I. Hedges, Elaine. II. Silber, Julie, 1944–
III. Title.
HQ1418.F47   1987   306'.0973   87-13957

ISBN 0-913327-15-8
ISBN 0-913327-14-X (pbk.)

A one-hour companion film, "Hearts and Hands," produced and directed by Pat Ferrero, is available
for purchase or rental from Ferrero Films, 371 Twenty-ninth Street, San Francisco 94131.

The Quilt Digest Press
955 Fourteenth Street
San Francisco 94114

For those historians and lovers of quilts, in our past and present,
who have worked diligently to retrieve and record
the lives of the women who came before us and our rich quilt heritage.
And to those yet to come, with the hope that they will continue.

The concept for this book grew out of the research for the film "Hearts and Hands."
This research was conducted over a seven-year period (1980–1987) and was in great part supported by funds from
the National Endowment for the Humanities/Public Media, the Rockefeller Foundation and *Quilter's Newsletter Magazine.*
This support is gratefully acknowledged.

Special thanks to those friends and colleagues who so generously extended both hearts and hands to this project.
For their counsel, information and support, we thank:

Cuesta Benberry
Inez Brooks-Myers
Mimi Carruthers
Ricky Clark
Diane Davenport
Tracy Gary

Francie Kendall
Michael Kile
Kate and Joel Kopp
Judy Mason
Harold Nadel

We also gratefully acknowledge the generous assistance of:

American Quilt Study Group
Nancy EV Bryk
Brad Bunnin
Laura Butler
Centralia (Illinois) Public Library
Nancy Druckman
David Duniway
Martha Frankel
Sally Garoutte
Laura Graham
Virginia Gunn
Kayo Hatta
Jonathan Holstein
Laurel Horton

Dean Johnson
Mary Lohrenz
Martha Mayo
Marsha McCloskey
Peter Palmquist
Linda Reuther
Sharon Risedorph
Merry Silber
Louise Steinman
Blair Tarr
Ann Troianello
Gail van der Hoof
Michael Vitucci

—*Pat Ferrero*
Julie Silber

Elaine Hedges wishes to give special thanks to:
Emily Daugherty, for her expert secretarial help;
Abby Markowitz and Elizabeth McHale, for their research assistance;
Judith Beris-Markowitz, Virginia Gunn and Julie Roy Jeffrey, for generously sharing their scholarship;
and William L. Hedges, for his sensitive reading of the manuscript and valuable critical advice.

Patriotic, by Elizabeth Holmes, location unknown, 1869, 90 × 71 inches, pieced and appliquéd cottons. Collection of Bill and Maggie Pearson.

*E*lizabeth Holmes's quilt leaves little doubt as to her political sentiments and point of view. Dated four years after Lincoln's assassination and the end of the Civil War, it reflects the continuing primacy of those traumatic events and the importance of large political issues in the lives of American women. In addition to memorializing Lincoln, in her quilt Elizabeth Holmes cast her ballot in the only way she could, celebrating the 1868 election of **GRANT PR**(esident), **COLFAX VI**(ce President), and **THE UNION FOREVER**.

WHEN NINETEENTH-century women described their quilts as "bound volumes of hieroglyphics" or as their "albums" and their "di'ries," they were fully aware of what we have recently newly recognized: that their stitched fabrics were often the most eloquent records of their lives.[1] Today we are in the midst of an explosion of interest in women's history, and historians, traditionally attracted to the written word as the way of understanding the past, are increasingly recognizing the need to turn to other sources as well, since women, who were often denied education and discouraged from writing, left fewer written records than men. One source, and a paramount one, is their quilts. For if comparatively few women wrote, practically all of them sewed, and in their quilts, especially, they found a capacious medium for expression. For vast numbers of nineteenth-century women, their needles became their pens and quilts their eminently expressive texts.

These texts have begun to be read, but primarily as products of the home environment, artifacts that illuminate the female life cycle and the domestic world inside which they originated.[2] The child's *Nine Patch,* the young woman's friendship, engagement and bridal quilts, the crib quilts of motherhood and the widow's quilts of bereavement served women as symbolic objects that ritualized and gave dignity to individual lives and that united women in ties of work and creative expression. Now, however, another important chapter is beginning to unfold, one that reveals women throughout the nineteenth century using their quilts as expansive fabrics on which they inscribed not only a personal but a public narrative as well: women used their quilts to register their responses to, and also their participation in, the major social, economic and political developments of their times. Through their quilts women became, in fact, not only witnesses to but active agents in important historical change.

Textiles, and women's changing relation to their time-honored textile work, provide indeed an essential thread for understanding women's complex roles in nineteenth-century history. To look at women's history through their quilts and their quilt work is to see the nineteenth century from a new perspective. In the pre-industrial, agricultural world that still prevailed in the century's opening decades and that would persist on successive frontiers, young girls still learned, at home and in school, those sewing and quilting skills that would fit them for their traditional adult domestic roles. The coming of industrialization and the rise of technology began to change that world, as textile work, and women with it, moved out of the home into the factories, and as a new ideology of domesticity, in which sewing played a significant part, emerged in reaction to women's changing status. The history of the century was also drastically shaped by the cotton economy of the pre–Civil War South, where textile work bound together with complex ties black slave and free white women; and by the great successive waves of westward migration, where quilts became, for pioneer women, agents of physical and psychological survival as well as of their civilizing mission in their new frontier homes. Throughout the century, women used their quilts and other textile products to help create for themselves a new, more public, role. From their church and missionary work through their participation in Civil War relief to their work in such major reform movements as abolition and temperance, women used their sewing and quilting skills to assert their agency in the world outside the home, to claim and secure for themselves more public and political space. If, by the end of the century, in the suffrage movement, quilts had become a problematic and ambivalent symbol of women's status, they had by then served a most important purpose. From being expressions of women's private lives, testaments to their domestic allegiance, quilts had also become in the course of the century political emblems and acts that helped women to expand their world and thus to negotiate their transition into modern times.

The U.S. Sanitary Commission was organized during the Civil War to work with the War Department to provide desperately needed supplies and medical care for Union soldiers. Women, by then already well organized in sewing and relief-work associations, formed the core and the leadership of this remarkably efficient and successful effort. When the war ended, returning soldiers received much-needed assistance in re-entering civilian life from the Soldiers' Aid Society, a branch of the U.S.S.C. It is interesting to note that, in a later drawing of this photograph (an exact replica of the image in every other way), the women who directed and operated the office (in the doorway) were completely removed. ‹To view the drawing, see Mary Clark Brayton and Ellen F. Terry, Our Acre and Its Harvest: Historical Sketch of the Soldiers' Aid Society of Northern Ohio *(Cleveland: Cleveland Branch of the United States Sanitary Commission, 1869), frontispiece.* ›

Vintage photograph of the United States Sanitary Commission and Soldiers' Aid Society storefront, 95 Bank Street, Cleveland, Ohio, c. 1865. Collection of The Western Reserve Historical Society, Cleveland.

Vintage photograph of suffragists on parade, New York City, May 16, 1912. Collection of the Library of Congress, Washington, D.C.

Equal suffrage was only one component of a multifaceted nineteenth-century woman's rights movement. The vote became an issue for women by the middle of the nineteenth century. By century's end, suffragists had taken to the streets to inform the public and to make demands. There was great energy and enthusiasm in these demonstrations, where women of mixed generations, with babies and banners, expressing shared commitments, marched together.

*I*n nineteenth-century America, women of every age, class, racial and ethnic background sewed. But an accurate and well-balanced represen-tation of that history is made extremely difficult by the lack of textile and photographic evidence of poor white women and women of color. In two decades of research, quilt historian Cuesta Benberry, for example, has un-covered very few surviving, well-documented slave quilts. Quilts made by poor people were of necessity used, often worn out completely. Overlooked, or until recently considered less important than textiles made by white middle- and upper-class women, very few quilts made by women of color (and photographic documentation of them) have survived. Thus, this image is extremely rare.

Vintage photograph of women and children near Thomasville, Georgia, c. 1890.
Collection of the Hargrett Rare Book & Manuscript Library, University of Georgia Libraries (negative number 944), Athens.

The Woman's Christian Temperance Union, founded in 1874, grew to be the largest women's organization of the nineteenth century and a major national political force. By 1907, the organization boasted 350,000 members from all over the country and dealt with a broad range of women's issues. This quilt, made before the turn of the century, symbolizes the W.C.T.U. in several ways. With the organization's initials embroidered in its official colors, it is an emblematic flag or banner. It also serves as a membership roster with Connecticut chapters and leaders' names inked or embroidered on the quilt blocks. Women from a variety of backgrounds were inspired to come together to create this quilt, which is said to have been presented as a gift/tribute to the charismatic longtime leader of the W.C.T.U., Frances Willard.

Shoo Fly, by Connecticut W.C.T.U. members, 1887, 73 × 72 ½ inches, pieced silks and taffetas, with embroidery and ink work. Collection of the National Woman's Christian Temperance Union, Evanston, Illinois.

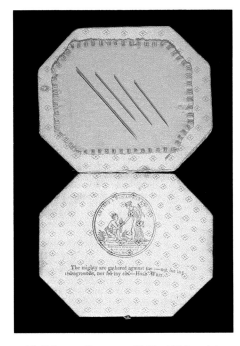

Abolition needle case, c. 1830–1850, origin unknown, 4 ½ × 3 ½ inches. Collection of the Essex Institute, Salem, Massachusetts.

Women became actively involved in the struggle to end slavery early in the 1830's. It was then, with abolition, that women first went beyond the voluntary missionary and charity work they had been doing since the beginning of the century to organize around larger social-reform issues. From the start, there had been an integral link joining sewing, organization and reform work. With abolition, we see the coming together of sewing and protest. Needle cases bore popular abolitionist slogans. This one reads: "AM I NOT A WOMAN AND A SISTER?"; "Remember them that are in bonds as bound with them. Heb. 13:3."; and "The mighty are gathered against me:—not for my transgression, nor for my sin. —HOLY WRIT."

A T THE BEGINNING of the nineteenth century, the United States was still an agricultural society, and vast numbers of women performed the age-old, pre-industrial tasks associated with textiles. They planted and grew flax and cotton, spun thread, wove cloth, and sewed the garments, household linens and bed quilts that were either necessary for the survival or desirable for the comfort of a family. The farm home was a domestic manufactory, where all family members were workers, and women were partners with men in the economic enterprise of supporting a family. The thread, cloth and clothing, the table and bed linens and quilts they produced were essential goods, as were the soap and candles they made, the fruits and vegetables they grew, and the foods they preserved. In this pre-industrial world, children learned at home, from parents and other adults, the work skills that would fit them for their future roles. "Home was then the school of 'Domestic Art,'" wrote a Blue Ridge, Virginia, plantation woman of her childhood in the 1830's and 1840's, and women's memoirs, diaries and autobiographies are replete with descriptions of their domestic training.[3]

Sewing, as an essential skill, was taught to children as young as two or three, or as soon as their fingers could grasp a needle. What they learned was "plain sewing"—such stitches as the basic running stitch, the "over-and-over" or over-sewing stitch, the back stitch and the hem stitch— necessary for the seaming and hemming of clothing, for making quilts and household linens, and the basis also for the fancy or ornamental sewing that might occupy a woman's leisure time. To this training was usually added knitting, for the making of stockings, shawls, gloves and mittens; and darning, for the mending of garments and household goods. Long after industrialization had removed spinning and weaving from the home, children both in pioneer and in more heavily settled areas were still taught sewing, including patchwork, and extraordinary numbers were proficient by the age of

five. Edith White remembered that during her childhood in Nevada County, California, in the early 1860's, "Mother always bought needles and thread and dry goods, and put them to good use making clothes for the family and teaching my sister and me to sew. Before I was five years old I had pieced one side of a quilt, sitting at her knee half an hour a day, and you may be sure she insisted on tiny stitches." Clara Lenroot, who grew up in Wisconsin at about the same

A mong the earliest popular photographic processes, daguerreotypes came to America from France in 1839. As they required exposures of one minute or more, it is not surprising that daguerreotypes of babies are often out of focus. This one, of an infant posed upon a Rob Peter to Pay Paul quilt, gives a hint of the ritual importance of quilts in the life cycle. Quilts were made for babies at or before birth and to mark other important passages throughout life.

Daguerreotype of infant on quilt, c. 1845.
Collection of America Hurrah Antiques, New York City.

*T*he Mariner's Compass design is one which comes directly out of the concerns and observations of women's daily lives. The fabrics in this quilt indicate that it was made in the first half of the nineteenth century, when there were still whaling ships in New England and life revolved around the sea, a sea that brought exotic, imported fabric to American women.

time, remembered being taught at five "to knit and to sew, sitting by [mother's] side in my little chair, carefully overhanding patchwork, or knitting long strips for the garters worn in those days." And Charlotte Perkins Gilman, later to become an important feminist writer and lecturer, wrote of her Providence, Rhode Island, childhood, also in the 1860's, that "I was taught to sew before five, little patchwork squares, in the tiniest of 'over-and-over' stitches."[4]

In some families the fifth birthday became a special rite of passage. "On my fifth birthday," Florence Kniseley of York County, Pennsylvania, recalled, "I had finished all but three patches for a quilt and papa was so anxious that I should get it all done on that day that he said he would make one for me if I would make two; this we did and the quilt was completed." And in 1847 near Newark, New Jersey, Harriette Kidder recorded in her diary that her daughter Katy "has nearly completed her quilt.... She has pieced every block—put them all together in long strips & assisted in sewing together these strips." A month later, Mrs. Kidder held a party at which "a company of young ladies" quilted Katy's quilt and thus celebrated her "fifth birthday," as she underscored it in her diary.[5]

The method usually employed in teaching sewing and quilting was the "stint"—the assignment of a specific amount of work to be done each day. Stints were assigned for a variety of needlework tasks. "Stockings were made at home from yarn spun, doubled, twisted and wound in balls. The girls of the family were required to knit a certain number of rounds each night before going to bed," reported a woman of her childhood in North Carolina in the 1830's. In the 1850's Caroline Cowles Richards of Canandaigua, New York, wrote in her diary that "I am sewing a sheet over and over for grandmother and she puts a pin in to show me my stint, before I can go out to play. I am always glad when I get to it." And Helen Doyle similarly described her childhood in upstate New York in the 1870's: "Grandmother cut and basted blocks of cloth for me and every day I must sew one square of nine blocks before I was free to play."[6]

The procedure of completing a specified amount of work rather than working for an arbitrary length of time seems to have been favored by mothers and grandmothers, as greater inducement to accomplishment and as encouraging a sense of achievement. Certainly Caroline Stickney, made to sew for an hour every afternoon in the 1850's—"generally 'over-and-over,' the seams of a sheet or blocks for a bed-quilt"—found that when the work became a question of time it was "unbearable." The stint allowed the child some sense of control; she could, within limits, choose when to do the work. And mothers and grandmothers provided other incentives to make the work enjoyable. Women recalled with pleasure being allowed to make a cradle quilt for a young sister or brother, or a doll quilt, of being allowed to add stitches to a mother's quilt, of having their work praised and displayed. "My mother was very proud of my quilt work and exhibited it at every opportunity," wrote Ann Johnson of her pioneer childhood in Texas; and perhaps that praise was not unrelated to her further saying that "I have kept up my quilt making all my life, and no other hand work is so interesting to me."[7]

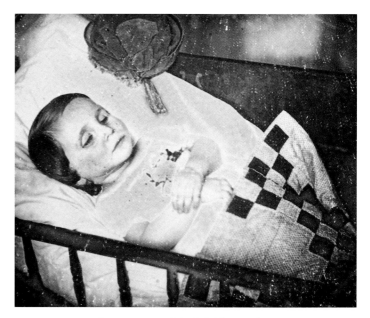

Daguerreotype of dead child, c. 1845.
Collection of The State Historical Society of Wisconsin, Madison.

*T*his early image, along with the one on page 16, captures the essence of quilts in people's lives. The introduction of the daguerreotype gave nineteenth-century Americans a new form of memorial and a way of keeping deceased loved ones close at hand and in mind. After the introduction of the daguerreotype, it became fashionable to capture the last physical reality of a loved one in a photograph just prior to burial. The quilt, that soft and tender and most personal of objects, accompanied Americans from cradle to grave.

Vintage photograph of young girls with their dolls, c. 1890.
Collection of America Hurrah Antiques, New York City.

*I*n the traditional gift of a doll to her daughter, a woman passed along far more than the small present itself; she was quietly transmitting her own values to her child as well as preparing the girl for future life. Through their dolls, "little mothers" began to gain basic sewing skills as well as a sense of what society would expect from them as women. This socialization, achieved through needlework training, was passed on from mother (or aunt or grandmother) to daughter, generation to generation, in a continuous female legacy.

were made to learn tailoring as a trade, she rebelled against the idea that "the chief end of woman was to make clothing for mankind." [9] Some young children— among them Frances Willard, later to be the leader of the Woman's Christian Temperance Union—protested the sedentary, confining nature of sewing, which kept her from the outdoor activity she loved; others resented its interference with intellectual ambition. Mary Livermore, Civil War relief worker, temperance and suffrage leader, was sent as a young girl in the 1830's to "a private school of superior quality" in Boston that offered reading, writing, arithmetic, a little geography, some "diluted" grammar—and "two hours of daily instruction in needlework." The sewing, she said, frayed her nerves as badly as it did the cloth, and she saw it as intruding upon the academic work she preferred.[10] That despite their antipathy to sewing all three of these women—Larcom, Willard and Livermore—would later find themselves famous for activities that importantly involved textile work is more than an irony of their individual lives: it is an index to the pervasiveness of textile-associated activities in nineteenth-century women's history.

Despite the protestations of young girls like Livermore, until well into the century the limited schooling that was available to girls and young women was intended to fit them not for careers or intellectual pursuits but for their domestic role—their future lives as wives and mothers. Sewing was therefore a standard part of the curriculum, often taking precedence over more academic subjects. Until the 1830's and 1840's, formal educational opportunities for females were on the whole confined to dame schools and elementary schools and, for the daughters of the well-to-do, private boarding or finishing schools. Dame schools were established in colonial New England for very young children and persisted into the early decades of the nineteenth century, moving west with the settlers. Lucy Larcom attended such a school at the age of two, and later recorded that "We learned to

Not all children, of course, responded so positively. Thorough training meant that children had to rip out and redo crooked, loose, or otherwise faulty stitches, and many women painfully recalled patchwork "smudged and blackened" from being worked and reworked, or knitting "soiled with constant handling by dirty fingers." [8] Others chafed at the restrictions such sewing imposed on body and mind, or resisted the role indoctrination into marriage and motherhood it represented. Thus, Lucy Larcom, growing up in Beverly, Massachusetts, in the 1820's, enjoyed arranging the fabrics for a patchwork quilt because the "little figured bits of cotton cloth" became a kind of visual poetry, suggesting loving familial associations. But she could not, or would not, create a quilt from the patches such as, she recorded, other children her age were doing, "with an eye to future housekeeping." And when she and her older sisters

Eagle, c. 1840–1860, Ohio, 90 × 90 inches, appliquéd cottons. Collection of Linda Reuther, Julie Silber/Mary Strickler's Quilt.

*P*atriotism was a major theme in nineteenth-century American life, and women expressed it in a glorious assortment of ways in their quilts. A popular Federalist symbol, the eagle appears on many late eighteenth- and early nineteenth-century quilts, and again just prior to the Civil War.

sew patchwork while we were learning the alphabet"; and Mary King in the same decade in Vermont remembered that all the girls carried their patchwork to school, "and the teacher was expected to see that it was well done." In the South the situation was similar. A woman who described her childhood on a North Carolina plantation recalled attending school at five, learning to read and to sew, and being "required to show to the visitors what sewing we had done."[11]

For large numbers of female children, especially those in rural areas, formal schooling was limited to the dame school, plus perhaps some "after hours" or summer sessions at an elementary or grammar school when it was not being used by the boys for whom it was primarily intended. The more fortunate daughters of affluent parents might attend the private finishing or boarding schools that flourished in the late eighteenth and early nineteenth centuries. Here, too, sewing was an essential component of the curriculum, but what was taught, especially in the southern states, was not plain sewing but ornamental needlework, "the most important discipline of a fashionable education."[12] The Grimké sisters, Angelina and Sarah, who would become important speakers in the abolitionist movement, attended such a school in Charleston. Reading, writing and enough arithmetic for man-

Detail of original design quilt, by a member of the Logan family, South Carolina, c. 1835–1855, now in the form of a runner 201 × 17¼ inches, appliquéd cottons. Collection of the Charleston Museum, Charleston, South Carolina.

Here an early quiltmaker has created a fabric record of a particular geographic place and time, a kind of map of her world. This detail is one section of several from a disassembled quilt which have been reorganized into a long narrative runner visualizing the Charleston of the quiltmaker's day. In a panorama of her town, she illustrated Charleston harbor itself and several different sailing ships. In the section illustrated here, she depicted the architecture of particular houses and poured out the contents of the homes in a kind of archaeology of daily life. Here is a personally observed, appliquéd inventory. These items, as well as the elegant fabrics from which they were sewn, reflect a very refined life. The quilt parallels the drawings and paintings of like scenes generally made by men of the era. This quiltmaker used the materials and techniques she knew and with which she had been socialized to create a rare, representational fabric interpretation of her personal environment.

aging a home were taught, plus French, some painting and music, and needlework: "white on white, stitchery and cross stitch...fancywork, beadwork, silk on velvet."[13] At northern academies, such as Sarah Pierce's famous Litchfield Female Academy in Connecticut, which was attended by both Catharine Beecher, who would become a women's education reformer, and Harriet, her sister, who, as Harriet Beecher Stowe, would become famous for *Uncle Tom's Cabin*, the curriculum emphasized more solid academic subjects, but both plain and ornamental sewing were also taught.

Litchfield Academy was a forerunner of the seminary or academy movement that signaled a major advance in the 1820's and 1830's in the quality of women's education. With the establishment of such schools as Emma Willard's Troy Female Seminary in 1821, Catharine Beecher's Hartford Female Seminary in 1823, and Mary Lyon's Mt. Holyoke Female Seminary in 1836, more systematic intellectual training became available. The westward expansion of the United States was opening up teaching as an occupation for women, and the new seminaries were also interested in training women to be missionaries, or missionaries' wives. While the new schools did not teach sewing, they were unanimous in agreeing that both the theory and practice of domestic economy were essential to a young woman's education. Woman's primary mission was still to be a wife and mother, and her true fulfillment would occur inside the home.

Indeed, by the 1830's woman's "mission" in the home was being newly emphasized. The decades from the 1830's through the 1860's saw the emergence of what has been termed "the cult of true womanhood" or "the cult of domesticity," an ideology that proffered a new and more rigorous definition of woman's role and place in society. The ideology was a conservative reaction to profound changes that were by then occurring, primary among them the development of industrialization. As the United States began

From the Revolutionary War onward, young girls attending dame schools, academies and many public schools were taught sewing skills as part of their essential curriculum. These girls look as if they are tied to their chairs, and this photograph gives a strong sense of what was, for some women, a tyranny of the needle—the forced inculcation of values through sewing. "(The schoolmaster) would not permit his female pupils to cipher in 'Fractions.' It was a waste of time, wholly unnecessary, would never be of the least use to them. If we could count our beaux and our skeins of yarn, it was sufficient." ‹Sarah Ann Emery, Reminiscences of a Nonagenarian *(Newburyport, Mass.: William H. Huse & Co., 1879), p. 49.›*

Vintage photograph of girls in classroom, c. 1890–1900. Collection of Pilgrim/Roy Antiques, San Francisco.

Daguerreotype of woman with quilt block, c. 1850.
Collection of America Hurrah Antiques, New York City.

to transform itself from an agricultural into an urbanized and industrialized nation, with families moving into the developing cities and towns, and men moving into wage work in the new commercial and industrial enterprises, woman's traditional pre-industrial role of producer of essential goods began to disappear. It is important to realize that the industrial revolution in the United States began with the removal from the home of some of women's time-honored textile work: spinning and weaving were the first work processes to be mechanized, and cloth became factory-produced. Later, other of women's traditional work activities would be removed from the home to the factory—preserving and canning, and baking, for example. Although at the beginning of the industrial revolution the large majority of American women continued to live inside a farm economy, for women in urban areas, economic dependence upon a husband's or a father's earnings increasingly became the rule. It was to such women, primarily northeastern native-born white women who were becoming deprived of their traditional work, that the cult of domesticity addressed itself. As historians have

recognized, however, such women set the cultural patterns for American women's self-definition, and in time the new ideology established norms against which all American women were expected to measure themselves.[14]

The new ideology defined women as innately different from men—intellectually inferior, more submissive and retiring, purer, more pious and morally sensitive, and "by nature" domestic and maternal. Given these unalterable differences, woman was to inhabit and confine herself to her own separate and distinct "sphere," that of the home. Within the home she was to fulfill certain essential functions: to uphold morality against the encroachments of the materialism, competitiveness and greed of the new commercial and industrial world; to create the home as a peaceful and soothing retreat from that world; and especially to devote herself to raising her children, for whose psychological and moral well-being she was increasingly seen as primarily—even solely—responsible. This private world of the home, it was argued, should give women sufficient scope for their abilities and sufficient satisfaction. The public world of trade and business, politics and governance, was for men.[15]

The cult ideology was disseminated by means of a vast body of prescriptive literature—advice books, volumes of sermons and essays, articles and specialized ladies' magazines, all designed to supply young girls, wives and mothers with what they needed to know in order properly to inhabit their ordained sphere. The literature dealt with such subjects as domestic economy, woman's wifely and maternal duties, her religious and charitable responsibilities, her eti-

Vintage photograph of the Stewart family, Spokane, Washington, July 5, 1889, by Milton Loryea. Collection of Peter Palmquist, Arcata, California.

quette and proper manners. Sewing was a subject of discussion in every category, and it came to represent such an array of both essential and desirable skills, habits, attitudes and virtues as to become the quintessential "feminine" activity, the one through which a woman most closely identified herself with her "sphere."

A composite of the discussions of sewing by the best-known authors of the advice literature would show that sewing was encouraged, and even prescribed, as domestic obligation, as creative opportunity, as the source of virtue, and as the exemplum of good manners. The earliest advice literature underscored the practical necessity of knowing how to sew in order to provide for one's family; in addition, in accordance with the Protestant work ethic, women were encouraged to "improve" their time, that is, to put all spare moments to useful purpose. Patchwork, in the early years of the cult, was especially favored as an example of such improving industriousness and even became the ideal metaphor for the diligent housewife. "The true economy of housekeeping,"

We have the names of each member of the family in this extraordinary photograph, but we have no other documented information about them. Nonetheless, the image itself provokes questions and suggests many issues. Had Mrs. Stewart been widowed early, as was common throughout the century? If so, how did she support her eight young children? What kinds of work would she be able to find?

The size of the brood and Mrs. Stewart's weary expression suggest to us the question of family planning, but it must be remembered that sexually related topics were very slow in surfacing as acceptable items for discussion. It was not until early in this century that contraception began to be privately and publicly discussed and to be seen as not only a personal but as a political and economic issue for women.

Crazy, c. 1890–1910, origin unknown, 65 × 65 inches, embroidered silks, velvets and taffetas.
Collection of Al and Merry Silber.

*T*his quilt reflects many of the changes which had taken place in women's lives in the nineteenth century. By the time this quilt was made, the role of many middle- and upper-class white women had shifted from essential producers of goods in the home to that of consumers for and moral protectors of it. Now many of these women, no longer involved in essential work in the home, were much affected by popular magazines such as Peterson's Magazine *and* Godey's Lady's Book, *which urged them to make highly embellished, non-utilitarian display pieces like this quilt. These quilts were decorative, reflecting Victorian taste and the status of the quiltmakers' husbands. Women had become symbols of leisure; to have a wife who was leisured reflected very favorably on a man.*

During this time, quilts were no longer found exclusively in the bedroom; typically we see them in the parlor, where art and music and women's "civilizing" influences could be practiced and displayed. Hundreds of thousands of quilts of this style were made between 1876 and 1920, many from pre-packaged collections of fancy scraps. These kits, sold through magazines from as early as 1884, often included suggested embroidery patterns, and as such represent a very conventionalized trend in quiltmaking. The example shown here, while definitely of the style, is distinguished from many by its inventiveness.

Lydia Child said in *The American Frugal Housewife* in 1829, "is the art of gathering up all the fragments so that nothing be lost. I mean fragments of *time* — as well as *materials*." Child emphasized that children especially should be taught patchwork as a way of making them "useful" at an early age. Lydia Sigourney in *Letters to Young Ladies* in 1833 and Eliza Leslie in *The Behavior Book* in 1859 agreed.[16] Patchwork, as well as other forms of plain sewing, taught neatness (a virtue that was particularly emphasized in the advice literature) and habits of attentiveness; sewing taught patience, the acceptance of repetition and routine; it fostered attitudes of selflessness and service to others, important since women were expected to sew not just for their families but for the poor and for the churches. Sewing also helped develop proper decorum. A young girl quietly absorbed in her sewing became, in the advice literature and in the popular fiction of the period as well, an image of the "modesty," the "quiet and retiring manners" that women were encouraged to develop.[17] ("Immodest" women were those crusading feminists like Mary Wollstonecraft or Frances Wright who spoke in public and wrote books agitating for female equality.) Sewing was also advocated for its "soothing and sedative effect.... It composes the nerves, and furnishes a corrective for many of the little irritations of domestic life." [18] And finally, sewing, especially ornamental sewing which was encouraged if done in moderation, could express a woman's taste, and a home tastefully embellished with the products of woman's needle would have an uplifting influence on its inhabitants. No wonder then that women read, in 1836, that sewing was the "truly feminine employment"; in 1858, that it "has ever been the appropriate occupation of woman"; and in 1859, that it was "essential to a woman's happiness, no less than her usefulness in accomplishing [the] mission of her life." [19] By 1868, when Sarah Josepha Hale, editor of the influential *Godey's Lady's Book,* announced that not to sew was to be "unfeminine," the meaning of sewing had shifted: from being a useful, practical skill (which some boys

The lives of the ordinary women of the last century are being pieced together from the fragments, written and otherwise, that they have left us. Unpublished diaries, such as this one, are now considered precious documents. In them, women who came before us pass on to us, in their own words, the texture of everyday life in small-town America. This diary is full of observations about the weather, reports of the diarist's employment in a small midwestern store and a revealing inventory of her domestic activities, which included visiting the sick, washing and ironing, as well as sewing and quilting (both often done with others); the author continually mentions quilting and sewing.

Diary of Lizzie Barnett, Cobb, Illinois. Collection of Cuesta Benberry.

Vintage photograph of quiltmakers, friends and relations, c. 1890–1910. Collection of Glendora Hutson.

also learned), it had become a way of socializing females into a narrowly defined and arbitrarily gendered notion of "femininity."[20]

The advice literature was widely read, with some books going into thirty or forty printings, and scholars are still debating its implications for women. In defining wifehood and motherhood as woman's ordained roles and the home as her appointed sphere, the cult circumscribed women more narrowly than had been the case in pre-industrial life, where they frequently engaged in trade and ran businesses. And it simultaneously stigmatized as deviant entire groups of women—those who remained unmarried, working women, slave women, immigrant women and those involved in the newly emerging movement for woman's rights.[21] On the other hand, it led women, living as the majority of them perforce did inside a female world, to develop deep ties of friendship and solidarity with each other and a sense of themselves as a distinct, and distinctive, group. This emergent group consciousness, supported as it was by the cult's definition of women as purer and more morally sensitive, soon began to encourage them to extend the boundaries of their sphere. As moral custodians, they argued, it was their responsibility to improve not just the home but the outside world as well. The participation of large numbers of women in the major reform movements of the century—abolition, temperance and suffrage—would be fueled by the cult's ascription to them of a redemptive role.

Meanwhile, the cult clearly created a cultural context inside which quilts could flourish. As historian Nancy Cott has observed, the cult "created great expectations in and of women to excel in their vocation," and quilts can be seen as a paramount expression of that desire to excel.[22] Both the work processes and the purposes of quilts, as Lydia Child indicated, fulfilled cult ideals: the frugal and industrious use of scraps both of fabric and time, and the crea-

tion of a practical and beautiful product that embodied women's role of nurturing and serving others. By the same token (although at the other extreme, often, from scrap quilts), the cult encouraged the practice of creating quilts for ceremonial or ritualistic purposes—crib quilts, engagement and bridal quilts, friendship quilts, widows' or mourning quilts—out of which emerged some of the greatest needlework achievements of nineteenth-century women. Living their lives within the framework of the family, where births, marriages and deaths were primary occasions, women took the humble, utilitarian bedcover, intimately associated with all of these major biological and life cycle events, and transformed it into a celebratory or commemorative symbolic marker.

A ceremonial quilt like this one, which took many hundreds of hours and practiced skill to realize, would have been made by a woman of great leisure and considerable wealth. In the antebellum South, quilts such as this were sometimes made wholly or in part by specialized sewing slaves.

Broderie Perse, c. 1830–1840, Kentucky, 122 × 120 inches, appliquéd cottons. Techniques include trapunto and stipple quilting. Courtesy of America Hurrah Antiques, New York City.

Collage of photographs of pairs of needlewomen, Ashland, Ohio, c. 1850. Collection of The Ashland County Historical Society, Ashland.

*O*ne can see at a glance that this is a portrait of quite a different community of women from that on page 27. The difference in social standing is reflected in the clothing and formality of these Ashland photographs. In the documentation that accompanies these images, the women are identified exclusively by their husbands' names and professions, such as Mrs. Major Fulkerson, Mrs. Dr. Kellogg or Mrs. Judge Wick; others are the wives of ministers, lawyers, bankers or the postmaster, all prominent men in the community. The documentation also tells us that the photographer was the husband of one of the women at whose home the group of forty met for a "carpet rag sewing session." Though it is not noted, this is the kind of gathering which could involve the voluntary benevolent activities in which such women commonly engaged.

View of the Boott Cotton Mills at Lowell, Mass., *wood engraving from Gleason's Pictorial, Boston, 1852.*
Collection of the Museum of American Textile History, North Andover, Massachusetts.

*L*owell was founded in 1826 by a group of Boston businessmen who came to Chelmsford, Massachusetts, and established several mills. The town was re-named for one of them, John Cabot Lowell, whose utopian fervor fueled visions of textile mills on the banks of the Merrimack River which would depart from old-world models and be mutually beneficial to themselves and their workers. At first, the new mills, set in idyllic landscaped grounds, provided both profit for the mill owners and agreeable working conditions for the young women who came to Lowell to improve their lives, seeking a respectable way to earn money. A planned environment with modern factories and boardinghouses, community and cultural programs, attracted the educated daughters of New England farmers who came in search of work to help support their families, send brothers to college, enhance their dowries or become independent. But the businessmen's idealism was short-lived. By 1834, working conditions had deteriorated and the "mill girls" had organized one of the first major industrial strikes in the United States, protesting a fifteen per cent reduction in their wages. The strike was not successful, but it became the basis of several well-organized female reform societies of the 1830's and 1840's, such as the Factory Girls Association and the Lowell Female Labor Reform Association.

I N ENCOURAGING WOMEN to stay at home, the cult was resisting the new industrial world, or positioning women as a bulwark against it. Meanwhile, that world was beckoning women to enter it, including some of the very ones that the cult addressed. As their traditional work of spinning and weaving was transferred to the factories, young women who were being deprived of that work in the home yet who remained skilled in it followed it into the new mills, where they became the first industrial workers.[23]

In the second quarter of the nineteenth century, the daughters of New England rural families were recruited into the textile mills that were being established along waterways in towns like Lowell and Lawrence in Massachusetts and Manchester in New Hampshire. They were attracted by wages superior to any they could earn through the few other kinds of paid work available to them—teaching, domestic work and sewing. And at Lowell, especially, they were attracted also by the amenities that were carefully provided to reassure them that as mill workers they would suffer no loss of social status—churches and libraries, schools and shops, and factories made to seem unthreatening by being tastefully set in landscaped grounds. These early "mill girls," as they were called, were a temporary source of supply, and the favorable working and living conditions they enjoyed were also temporary. Individually they worked in the mills between two and four years, and collectively they began by the 1840's and 1850's to be supplanted by a new labor force composed of French-Canadian and Irish immigrant women, men and children. By that time, market fluctuations in the price and supply of cotton had led to severely deteriorated conditions—speed-ups, pay cuts and worsening physical surroundings. Factory work was becoming exploited work, and native-born white women avoided it.[24]

Such worsening conditions indeed began to be evident as early as the 1830's, and the mill girls, who before had lived relatively quiet rural lives, responded by organized protest—they led the first massive in-

Daguerreotype of woman at machine, c. 1850. Collection of the Museum of American Textile History, North Andover, Massachusetts.

In 1850, photography was young. Time exposures of a minute of two were required, making interior photographs difficult and action photographs impossible. Inside the huge textile mills at Lawrence and Lowell, light was scarce and there were three hundred or more machines such as this one on each floor. But, fortunately, some photographer felt it was important enough to overcome these difficulties and single out a young working woman at her machine, leaving us a rare and important document. We tend to forget the magic and wonder of photography. Lucy Larcom, herself the subject of a daguerreotype made around 1850, was amazed by the process, and she recalled a poem on how both a physical likeness as well as one's moral fiber seem to be captured on film: "It seemed almost too great a marvel to be believed. I saw some verses about it which impressed me much. . . . 'Oh, what if thus our evil deeds / Are mirrored on the sky / And every line of our wild lives / Daguerreotyped on high?'" ‹Lucy Larcom, A New England Girlhood (Gloucester, Mass.: Peter Smith, 1973), pp. 250–251.›

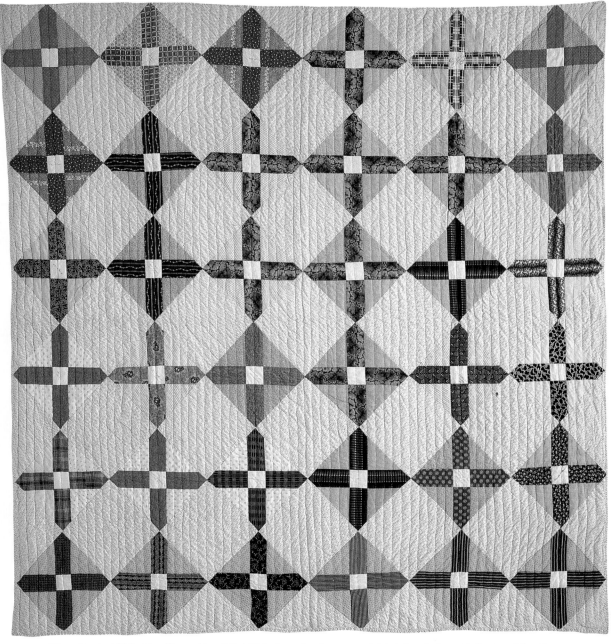

*F*riendship quilts, fabric versions of auto-graph albums, were made in great numbers between 1840 and the Civil War, a period of radical change and industrialization when many fami-lies were leaving New England and heading westward. Some of these pio-neers never saw friends or family again. The blocks on this quilt are signed by sixteen friends and rela-tives; one of the central blocks is in-scribed "Grand-mothers gift."

Album Patch, 1850, New Hampshire, 78 × 78 inches, pieced cottons, with ink inscriptions. Collection of Pat Ferrero.

dustrial walkouts, strikes and shutdowns in the United States, and in 1845 they formed the Female Labor Reform Association at Lowell to agitate for a ten-hour working day. Although their efforts failed to halt the trend towards increasing exploitation of fac-tory workers, they did cause the first governmental inquiry ever to be held to investigate labor conditions in the United States, and they demonstrated, as one historian has said, "that factory women could exert influence beyond their limited sphere."[25] The mill girls were also actively involved in political reforms. They attended lectures given by prominent reform-ers, including the abolitionist poet John Greenleaf

Whittier, dress reformer and woman's rights advocate Amelia Bloomer and Angelina and Sarah Grimké, Quaker abolitionists. When the Boston Female Anti-Slavery Society sponsored the Grimkés' seventeen-city abolitionist tour of 1837, almost two thousand people appeared for their lecture in Lowell. In addi-tion, many of the mill girls signed anti-slavery peti-tions presented to Congress; "In April of 1838 the bundles of abolition petitions presented and tabled at that session filled a room 20 × 30 × 14 feet, closely packed to the ceiling."[26]

The experience of the New England mill girls was also of historical significance in that it marked the

The early friendship quilt from which this detail is taken has blocks which provide anecdotal images of ordinary New England life, like a ship, a beehive and a couple being married. The popularity of ink drawing immediately preceded the advent of photography and was a common way for untrained artists to make detailed observations of life around them. Such drawings appear, along with written messages, on many friendship quilts of the period. This block, with a drawing of a man working at a textile machine, is likely a local observation: there were several large-scale textile mills in New Hampshire at the time this quilt was made. Each drawing in the quilt shares a block with imported printed fabric. Most American textile mills were producing large volumes of simple, utilitarian, unprinted cloth. Ironically, much of this New England–made fabric was shipped into the South to clothe the four million slaves who had picked the cotton from which it was woven.

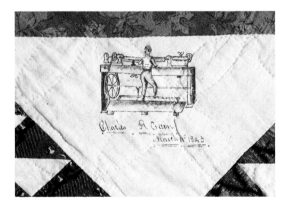

Detail of friendship quilt, c. 1842–1844,
probably New Hampshire, pieced cottons, with ink work.
Collection of Al and Merry Silber.

beginning of a major change in the relationship of women to their traditional textile work. Accustomed as they were to the dawn-to-dusk schedule of farm life, the mill girls may not have worked harder in the factories than they had at home, but the pace, the rhythms and the scheduling of their work were all different. From a task-oriented society, where human need determined when and how much work was done, and where work and social occasions could intermingle, as in the quilting bee, they moved into a work world ruled by clock time: by, that is to say, the mechanical regularities of the industrial world. At Lowell and elsewhere, this new work rhythm was

governed by bells. "Up before day, at the clang of the bell—and out of the mill by the clang of the bell—into the mill, and at work, in obedience to that ding-dong of the bell—just as though we were so many living machines."[27]

For the youngest workers, girls of ten or eleven who were employed as "doffers" to remove and replace bobbins on the spinning machines, work was less demanding—fifteen minutes out of each hour perhaps, with the rest of the time free for reading or sewing. Lucy Larcom was such a doffer, arriving at the Lowell mills in 1835 with her widowed mother and her sisters. Larcom lived through many of the changes that would characterize women's lives in the nineteenth century. From a pre-industrial rural childhood she moved to factory labor and then for a period of time to a pioneering life with her sister on the Illinois frontier. Her depiction of life in Lowell in the autobiography she wrote late in her life is imbued with nostalgia. Nevertheless, she conveys her sense, if not of being a "living machine," then of being surrounded by machinery: the "unceasing clash of sound," the "unremitting clamor," the "buzzing and hissing and whizzing of pulleys and rollers and spindles and flyers." The noise suggests the scale of factory textile work, and that, as well as the mechanization, made for a radical difference in the relationship of the worker to her work. Regulated by the bells and by clock time, limited to and accountable for only a segment of the finished textile product, the worker might begin to feel that alienation from her work that would become increasingly characteristic of an industrial economy. Larcom herself, having worked in the spinning and dressing rooms, chose to transfer to the cloth room, where she earned lower wages but was free of "the bondage of machinery," worked in a space more scaled to human size and could exercise more personal control over her work, which was to measure and record in ledgers the amounts of finished cloth.[28]

In 1845, the year Larcom left the mills, *The Lowell Offering*, a literary journal that the mill girls wrote and produced, published an essay, "The Patchwork Quilt." It may have been written (its precise authorship is unknown) by one of the mill workers, Harriet Farley, who was already by then agitating for better working and wage conditions. The essay is among the earliest descriptions of quiltmaking in our literature, and it is both a celebration of and a eulogy to pre-industrial work processes. It describes a patchwork

Photographic portrait of Lucy Larcom, c. 1860.
Collection of the New Hampshire Historical Society, Concord.

quilt that its author worked on from childhood through adolescence to adulthood: the quilt represents her apprenticeship in sewing and her developing skill, her growth from youth to young ladyhood, through dreams of love and marriage, to the death of her sister. The textiles in the quilt, scraps of fabric from her own, her mother's, sister's, brother's and friends' clothing, transform it into a text that incorporates "passages of my life," "memories of childhood, youth, and maturer years ... of life and death." A lovingly handmade product, informed with feeling and expressive of organic life and work processes, the quilt implicitly comments on the impersonality and disjunctions of factory textile work. In describing it as a "precious reliquary" and herself as an "old maid," however, the author is already introducing into the quilt culture that note of nostalgia that would develop by the end of the century into a sustained lament for the passing of the pre-industrial way of life.[29]

MEANWHILE, OTHER DEVELOPMENTS were moving quiltmaking into the new world of commerce and technology. In the 1840's and 1850's there appeared in Baltimore, Maryland, a distinctive quilt type that in some aspects of its production process and design motifs was happily embracing the new commercial and industrial world. The Baltimore album quilts that were made at mid-century for ministers and teachers, brides and cherished friends were frequently constructed either wholly or in part of professionally designed blocks which seem to have been purchased or else commissioned by clients and custom-made for them. The entrance of a professional like Baltimore resident Mary Evans into quiltmaking was a new de-

Detail of quilt on page 35.

Album, probably by Mary Evans, Baltimore, Maryland, 1848, 108 × 108 inches, appliquéd cottons, with ink work. Inscribed to John and Rebecca Chamberlain. Collection of Linda Reuther, Julie Silber/Mary Strickler's Quilt.

W e know from the meticulous research of Dena Katzenberg that many Baltimore album quilts were made with some or all of the blocks designed by professional quiltmaker Mary Evans. What distinguishes this example is an overall and consistent brilliance to the needlework. In it, every block appears to be by one hand, probably that of Evans herself.

35

parture. By the 1840's, many individual women in villages and towns throughout the country may have been making quilts for sale, sporadically or regularly, as a source of supplemental income. Mary Evans's procedure, however, of supplying prefabricated blocks for which she received payment (and also of signing those blocks in a standardized script with their donors' names) suggests both the specialization of work of the new industrial world and the commercial methods of the urban merchants who were proliferating in Baltimore at the time.[30]

The new professionalism and specialization, however, did not wholly replace traditional quiltmaking processes. What is significant about the Baltimore album quilts is their happy blending of old and new quiltmaking methods and old and new design motifs. The professionally designed and manufactured blocks were often inserted into the grid structure of the album quilts alongside homemade blocks; and the design motifs also represented a joining of the pre-industrial and industrial worlds. Traditional floral wreaths and sprays, cornucopias and baskets of fruit and flowers make up most of the surface of the album quilts. Comfortably comporting with them are blocks containing ships and steam engines, urban buildings and civic monuments. Popular American culture in this time period widely celebrated the new technology through the image of "the machine in the garden": the prevailing belief was that industrialization would not destroy nature or disrupt the natural rhythms of life; the mechanical would not threaten the organic.[31] The Baltimore album quilts might be seen as the textile expression of this popular optimism.

The ebullience that is conveyed by the multifoliated and flower-bedecked, brightly colored and richly textured surfaces of the album quilts suited Baltimore, which in the 1840's was the largest seaport and the third largest city in the United States. Indeed, much of the city's prosperity was built on textile manufacture. Cotton production was Baltimore's, and the nation's, largest industry. The quality and the variety of the fabrics in the album quilts splendidly display the benefits of technological progress in textile production by mid-century. The sheer abundance of a variety of fabrics enabled a quiltmaker like Mary Evans to utilize twenty to thirty separate bits of fabric to compose a single flower; the technological progress in the manufacture of cloth by the 1840's—improvements in color and in printing quality—inspired and produced some of the extraordinarily realistic

Detail of album quilt, c. 1840–1850, Baltimore, Maryland area, appliquéd cottons, with ink work. Private collection. Photograph courtesy of Sotheby's, Inc., New York City.

In the 1840's, Baltimore was on the brink of full industrialization. The classic album quilts from that city reflect those times: they not only visualize and glorify technological innovations (such as in this quilt block with its appliquéd steam locomotive), but the quilts themselves sit midway between the old hand technology and mass production. We see a hint of the concept of an "assembly" process in the pre-cut blocks, prepared by a professional quiltmaker and purchased to be included in homemade quilts. The Baltimore quilts reflect an important change in the economic framework of quiltmaking as well as a shift in attitude and in a mode of thinking. Until this period, quilts had been made within families. Quilts were exchanges and gifts, the very personal expressions of individual quiltmakers. In Baltimore, we see a very significant shift to cash payment for quilts.

effects achieved in the quilts: imported lustre prints, rainbow prints and watered silks, but also the calicoes, checks and plaids of American manufacture were used to simulate everything from the rind of a watermelon to the lattice work of a basket to the speckled egg of a bird.[32] The album quilts are in their way a hymn to technological progress.

WITHIN ANOTHER TEN YEARS, American women were responding to yet another technological advance, the sewing machine. The sewing machine began to be widely produced by the late 1850's and early 1860's, and it was greeted with delight as a miraculous timesaver. One can understand why. Before the sewing machine was available, hand sewing might consume more hours of a woman's day than any other single task. One southern woman reported that her mother spent twelve hours a day on hand sewing in order to provide for her family and slave "servants," and another wrote, from her vantage point in the twentieth century, that "the overseaming, the hemming, the felling, the stitching and hemstitching, the buttonholing and quilting, the overcasting, running and darning that was done would appall the woman of today."[33] Both homemakers and reformers interested in reducing women's household drudgery therefore hailed the machine. Sarah Josepha Hale was an early champion, as was dress reformer Amelia Bloomer, who saw the machine as woman's "merciful" release from work that had "stitched her health and life away." And a Vineyard Haven, Massachusetts, woman, friend of woman's rights advocates

Photographer Butcher documented the settling of Nebraska in the 1880's with fifteen hundred portraits of frontier families. A folklorist ahead of his time, Butcher also collected the stories of life within the walls of the simple sod houses he photographed. Many of the families chose to drag their sewing machines outside for these portraits, a fact which says a great deal about how important that tool was to ordinary nineteenth-century Americans. The extraordinary sales of sewing machines in the Civil War period and the decades following foretell a growing consumerism and are proof of the "improved" marketing techniques of the period. Isaac Merrit Singer was an especially brilliant promoter of his product. He gave free sewing machines to many ministers' wives, knowing that, since those women were the arbiters of taste in America's small towns, the other women in the parishes would want machines, too. He was, of course, quite right: in 1858, Singer sold 3,591 machines; sales figures for 1870 had soared to 127,833 units!

An 1888 photograph of the W. H. Blair house at Huckleberry, near Broken Bow, Nebraska, by Solomon Butcher.
Solomon D. Butcher Collection/Nebraska State Historical Society, Lincoln.

Lucy Stone and Elizabeth Blackwell, purchased the first machine on her island in the 1860's as her way of demonstrating being a "progressive woman."[34]

Housewives shared the reformers' sentiments. To Harriette Kidder, who acquired her machine in 1859 and had by then five children to clothe, it was "a very valuable household article. It renders sewing a pleasure rather than a toil." Ann Johnson's husband surprised her with a sewing machine as a gift in the 1870's, and after her years of hand sewing it was, she said, "a wonder to us all." Elizabeth Welty, homesteading in Colorado in 1891, was determined that the family "thresh over 1600 bushels of wheat" so that "I can get a new sewing machine."[35] Where machines were scarce in pioneer regions, they were shared, with women visiting each other's homes and spending the night to get their sewing done. Those who owned machines found themselves teaching a flow of neighbors (and approving of those who were "apt scholars") and also demonstrating the machine to husbands who, after all, would usually be paying the purchase price.[36]

The time saved was indeed considerable. A Kansas woman in the 1860's estimated that she could sew more in a day on the new machine than in a week by hand, and Sarah Josepha Hale in *Godey's* argued that twenty hours of work could be done in two or three. Estimates by historians today are that a calico dress that took six and one-half hours by hand took fifty-seven minutes by machine, and a man's shirt one hour as opposed to fourteen.[37] Ironically, however, owning a machine could also tempt women to do more sewing rather than less. Ruth E. Finley, author of *Old Patchwork Quilts* and of a biography of Sarah Josepha Hale, observed that it encouraged women to produce fussier, more elaborate clothing, since the machine could make ruffles, pleats, tucks, puffs and "riotous trimming." By the time the sewing machine was being mass-produced for home use, factory sewing had begun to revolutionize the production of men's clothing: first military uniforms and then, after the Civil War, ready-made suits for middle- and working-class men. Later, children's clothing also became factory-produced. But until well into the 1890's women's dresses, with their complicated architecture of tight bodices, below-the-waist fittings and bustles, had to be made at home, with or without the help of a professional dressmaker.[38] The availability of the sewing machine may also have led women to do more hand sewing in the form of ornamental needlework.

This photograph beautifully illustrates the abundance of fabric available to women in the late nineteenth century. During the second half of the century, the printing and dyeing of cloth was undergoing a technological revolution. Not only did burgeoning industrialization and consumerism dramatically expand the "palette" and "vocabulary" of every quiltmaker, but the cheerful vibrancy of the new colors literally served as a psychological lifesaver to women living in bleak or isolated places.

Vintage photograph of dry goods store, Lakota, North Dakota, c. 1900. Collection of the State Historical Society of North Dakota (negative number A2831), Bismarck.

Amelia Bloomer hoped that by eliminating much utilitarian hand sewing the machine would liberate women into "more active and lucrative pursuits," but as early as 1859 Mrs. Pullan, English expert on needlework whose writings were published and widely read in this country, was offering a different definition of the sewing machine as the "Liberator of our sex." By using the machine to dispatch their necessary (and boring) plain sewing, she urged, women would have more leisure for hand-wrought fancy work. All women, and not just wealthy ones, could now cultivate those "accomplishments and charms" that had originally helped them win their husbands' hearts.[39]

Mrs. Pullan did not include quilts among women's "accomplishments." To make patchwork cushions, chair covers or ottomans out of bits of silk, velvet or satin was an acceptable "amusement," she wrote, but the calico quilt was a "valueless" use of woman's time.[40] Clearly, American quilters disagreed, and they proceeded to find the sewing machine a boon, a challenge and an inspiration. Some women celebrated the new machine by producing elaborate quilts that were testimonials to it and pyrotechnical displays of its capabilities. All-white quilts, avoiding the distractions of fabric pattern and color and of pieced designs, were especially favored as showing the possibilities of machine quilting as well as the maker's prowess at complex embellishment. The lavishness and complexity of such quilts suggests the ways in which the new machine stimulated the quiltmaker's imagination by providing new creative challenges. Of course machine stitching could also facilitate the work of piecing. Intricately pieced quilts in complex, graphic geometric patterns were made more simply and precisely with the aid of the machine. Quilt historian Jonathan Holstein claims that almost half of the quilts he has seen that were made after 1860 are machine-stitched.[41] Other quilt authorities believe the percentage is as high as seventy-five per cent of quilts made between 1860 and 1940. The machine's speed and its technical possibilities, combined with other developments in textiles and textile-related products—the availability of commercial cotton batting after 1850, aniline dyes, improved fiber quality, over twelve hundred shades of color in printed textiles by the 1870's and factory-manufactured hard twist cotton thread—constituted a complex of technological developments that could stimulate quilters and help make the second half of the nineteenth century, as Holstein has argued, "visually the most inventive" in American quiltmaking.[42]

Here is an example of how one late-nineteenth-century quiltmaker used the great variety of fabrics available to her. Technically, this is quite a simple quilt—a One Patch using the square over and over again. But this quiltmaker utilized a skillful understanding of color, delineating diagonals of various shades and hues, to make a quilt that is exemplary of the finest of the vibrant creations of its era.

One Patch, c. 1875–1900, found in Michigan, 80 × 80 inches, pieced cottons.
Collection of Linda Reuther, Julie Silber/Mary Strickler's Quilt.

J. & P. Coats trade-card poster, 1885, 13¼ × 28¾ inches.
Collection of Coats & Clark, Inc., Stamford, Connecticut.

*T*rade cards and posters, with advertisements for consumer items, were popular in the 1870's and 1880's and suggest the growing consumerism and marketing techniques of that period. This example, from J. & P. Coats, clearly visualizes the interconnections of the North and South in the cotton economy. The cotton thread is central in the image, with the source of the raw material (field labor) above, transportation below and the northern manufacture of the cotton into thread nearer the center. Even though this card postdates the legal emancipation of black Americans by two decades, it presents the disturbing stereotypical imagery of "happy darkies" that pervaded American society well into our modern day.

THE DARK UNDERSIDE of much of this technological progress, however, was the existence of slavery. It was southern cotton, grown by exploited slave labor, that was sent to the Rockland Print Works in Baltimore, eventually to make its way into the album quilts, and it was southern cotton that Lucy Larcom helped turn into cloth at Lowell. In the twenty years from 1840 to 1860, as demand increased and textile mills proliferated, the consumption of cotton in the United States quadrupled. The increased demand by both English and American industry led southern planters relentlessly to expand production, and the South became locked into a single-crop economy.[43] Under the rule of "King Cotton," women, northern and southern, were joined in painfully ironic ties. Lucy Larcom would express her anguished sense of this "bond" between northern mill and southern slave women in a Civil War poem she would write, where a mill worker on the banks of the Merrimack River sees the web she is weaving from slave cotton as a "hideous tapestry."[44] Cotton and textile work were the bonds that ambivalently united southern white

---

In the 1830's, when Lucy Larcom went to work in the textile mills at Lowell, Massachusetts, she was like the other recruits—young, literate daughters of New England farmers: she was looking to broaden her horizons and was open to new ideas. At Lowell she was exposed to abolitionist ideas in lectures given by social-reform leaders of the day, such as abolitionist poet John Greenleaf Whittier, who came to speak to the young mill workers. Larcom recognized a connection between her own labor and that of the black slave women who produced the raw materials she worked with; she expressed her ideas and feelings in this poem. The terms "slave wages" and "slave labor" had a special resonance for those mill girls who themselves would strike against wage cuts, for improved working conditions and for reduction of the twelve-hour day and six-day week.

· · ·

"I weave, and weave, the livelong day:
*   The woof is strong, the warp is good:*
I weave, to be my mother's stay;
*   I weave to win my daily food:*
But ever as I weave," saith she,
"The world of women haunteth me.

· · ·

"Wind on, by willow and by pine,
*   Thou blue, untroubled Merrimack!*
Afar by sunnier streams than thine,
*   My sisters toil, with foreheads black,*
And water with their blood this root,
Whereof we gather bounteous fruit.

"And how much of your wrong is mine,
*   Dark women slaving at the South?*
Of your stolen grapes I quaff the wine;
*   The bread you starve for fills my mouth:*
The beam unwinds, but every thread
With blood of strangled souls is red."

· · ·

‹ *Lucy Larcom,* Poems *(Boston: Fields, Osgood, & Co., 1869), pp. 134–137.* ›

Love Apple, by Mary Elizabeth Lyons, probably Kentucky, 1859, 108 × 98 inches, appliquéd cottons. Techniques include trapunto (note the pairs of hearts and clasped hands near the center) and embroidery. Collection of Alice Lee Harris.

This quilt, made in Kentucky (?) nearly a century and a half ago, remains in the family after five generations. Its condition, which is almost perfect, suggests the care and value given to such heirlooms. While the details of Mary Elizabeth Lyons's life are unknown, the quality and style of her quilt are typical of the kinds made by antebellum plantation mistresses. Most wives of planters were bred to excel in hospitality and domestic skills, living in comparative luxury. The ideal was refined gentility, but the reality was unremitting labor, which sometimes included sewing clothing for the slaves. The mistress "attends to all the spinning, weaving, and sewing. . . . She does more than any Northern woman I ever saw." ‹Sarah Frances (Hicks) Williams, Papers, 1838-68 [MS] (Chapel Hill: University of North Carolina Library, Southern Historical Collection), letter of February 3, 1855. ›

42

plantation and slave women as well. The lives of both groups revolved around the production of cotton, and making garments and bedding from the fiber was the regular and essential work of both.

Studying nineteenth-century women from the point of view of their textile work goes far towards disabusing us of certain myths and illusions we may have held about the southern white plantation mistress. Far from being a creature of leisure and lace, gauze and crinoline, she was often driven, harried and overworked. As a young woman in boarding school and as a wife she did produce the elegant needlework products for which she is famous—embroidered counterpanes, and quilts of appliqué and reverse appliqué, subtle colors and fine stitching. But, once married, she also assumed extensive responsibilities, including heavy amounts of both physical and managerial work. If, as one southern woman said, she was expected to be "an ornament to the drawing room," where she might do and display her needlework, she had "to be also equipped for taking charge of an establishment and superintending every detail of employment on a plantation."[45] The plantation mistress oversaw the food, clothing and health needs of both the slaves and her own family, and while she delegated cooking, cleaning and laundry to "servants," as the slaves were often called, she not only supervised the production of cloth, clothing and bedding but made a great deal of it herself. According to historian Catherine Clinton, the production of cloth and the manufacture of clothing was the plantation mistress's "most demanding task," and the production of linens, counterpanes and quilts was another primary responsibility. The lament of the overworked seamstress, Clinton says, was a common theme in southern women's letters.[46] Sarah Hicks Williams, a northern woman who married a North Carolina planter, certainly agreed. In a letter to her mother she described her own work in 1853: "At the moment there is sewing a plenty in hand for the Servants—at this season the Women have each a thick dress, chemise, shoes, a blanket given them, the Men pantaloons & jacket, shirt, blanket & shoes, besides caps & bonnets, the children too are clothed in the same

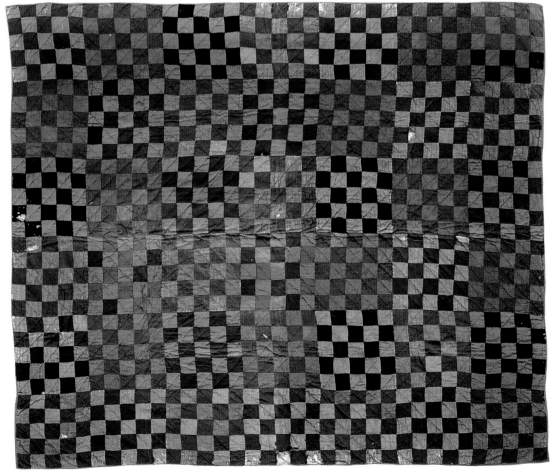

Twenty-five Patch, by Winny Rupe, Missouri, date unknown, 76 × 64 inches, pieced cottons and wools.
Collection of Dr. Henry Knock and Mrs. Cynthia Rupe Knock.

Winny Morton was born a slave in the 1850's. When she was about seven years old, she stowed away with a plantation visitor who was returning home to Missouri. Winny was delivered in Missouri to a friend of the visitor, Richard Rupe, whose family protected Winny from being returned to slavery. Winny was raised along with the Rupe children and took the family name. She was sent to school in a nearby town where, it was hoped, she would find black friends. But Winny preferred the Rupe farm and returned to stay as a beloved, free house servant until her death in 1947. She read voraciously, had her own bank account, was a locally renowned cook and made quilts.

materials—now many keep a Seamstress to do this, but Mother Williams [her mother-in-law, with whom she is living] has always done it herself with the assistance of her daughters when they were home, of course, I chose to do my part."[47]

On large plantations—those with over one hundred slaves—slaves were often trained for specialized work, which in the case of women meant spinning, weaving and sewing. A "sewing slave" worked in the Big House where she assisted the mistress and was often accomplished in fine needlework. One ex-slave described his mother's work under slavery as cutting and sewing the plantation clothes and then making quilts out of the scraps.[48] Sewing slaves were highly valued: they cost and were sold for more money. In 1858 Sarah Hicks Williams was delighted with the bargain her husband had made in paying "only one thousand dollars for a slave, Anarchy, who "can cut out pantaloons shirts & is a good sewer."[49]

However, large plantations with specialized help were not typical of the southern system. Seventy per cent of all slaveholders owned fewer than ten slaves, and the vast majority of the four million slaves who inhabited the South on the eve of the Civil War lived on small or moderate-size farms. Most slave women, therefore, like the men, worked in the fields by day: they ploughed, planted and picked the cotton, and they also chopped wood and rolled logs. In the evenings they then had to do all the domestic work for their families, with the result that their work "day" often stretched into the early hours of the morning, making it, historians agree, longer than that of the men.[50] All available evidence points to textile work as consuming the largest number of the slave woman's evening hours.

Even if their endless workday had somehow allowed time for writing, slaves were prohibited from acquiring literacy—learning to read and write were punishable crimes—and so we do not have many first-hand accounts of slave women's lives. Among our richest sources of information are the thousands of interviews with ex-slaves and their descendants that were conducted in the 1930's under the auspices of the WPA Federal Writers Project, and from these interviews one can piece together a picture of the kinds and amounts of slave women's textile work.[51] Some of it was imposed by the white mistress, including spinning anywhere from two to seven "cuts" of thread or yarn (a cut being one hundred turns of the wheel) and piecing quilts. One ex-slave described her

*H*ere is an example of a photograph which was made with a very specific purpose and inadvertently captures quite another essence. In March 1850, biologist Louis Agassiz commissioned a daguerreotypist to document first-generation and second-generation African slaves in South Carolina for a comparative study of the races. Judging by the quality of her dress, Delia, who lived on the plantation of B. F. Taylor in Columbia, South Carolina, likely was a house slave. The luxurious imported fabric in her dress is the kind which appears in elegant quilts of the period. The considerable status and privilege of her position as a house slave (relative to the field slaves), however, did not protect Delia from the humiliation of being stripped to the waist in front of an unknown man who was there to "inventory" her. The look on Delia's face clearly reveals the violation—the emotional truth of what it meant to have no control over one's own body, space or time.

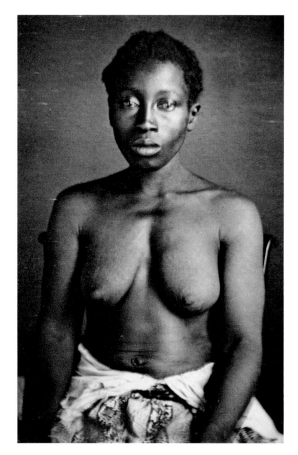

A March, 1850 daguerreotype of Delia by J. T. Zealy. Collection of The Peabody Museum, Harvard University (negative number N27531), Cambridge, Massachusetts.

childhood experience of helping her mother with her evening work of piecing and tacking quilts for the family's use and "for de white folks too." Children were routinely recruited to help their mothers, and in this case the narrator's brother scarred her arm when, sleepless and exhausted, he let fall the lighted pine knot he was holding, "all de light we ever had."[52] Making quilts for their own use was another primary task, since slaves usually had to supplement the meager supplies of bedding they received. Sarah Hicks Williams referred to "a blanket" being given to each slave, and another pre-war account states that "on very few estates are the colored people provided with any bedding; the best masters give only a blanket." A present-day historian says that bedding often consisted of only one light cotton blanket every third year.[53]

Much of the quilt work that slave women did therefore was intended to produce sturdy, utilitarian bedcovers, and in materials and construction it would not have been unfamiliar to poor white southern women, such as those in Appalachia. Tops were often made, as ex-slaves described, of "wore out clothes and breeches" which were "cut into squares and strips." The filling was also scrap: cotton picked from the ground in ginning time, wool removed from briar patches where sheep had passed through (and requiring hours of work to remove the burrs), or rags, old clothes and quilts too worn for further use.[54] Some women had access to finer materials, including scraps received from the white mistress and fabrics they might purchase themselves. Slaves could earn money by selling the produce from the garden plots they were sometimes given, the chickens and eggs they were allowed to raise, or the straw brooms they made; and skilled slaves, frequently hired out to other whites by their masters or mistresses, were sometimes allowed to keep some of the wages they earned. With this money they could buy material and piece quilts either for their own use or for sale.[55]

Some slave women were able to use their needlework skills to buy their freedom. Probably the best known of these is Elizabeth Keckley, who became seamstress to Mary Todd Lincoln. At one point in her life as a slave, Keckley supported seventeen people by her needlework skills, including the members of the family of her then-impoverished white owner. In 1855 she was able to buy her own and her mulatto son's freedom for twelve hundred dollars. The money was lent her by white society women in St. Louis for

Photographic portrait of Harriet Powers, c. 1890.
Collection of the Museum of Fine Arts, Boston, Massachusetts.

*N*ineteenth-century photographs of black women who are documented quiltmakers are very rare. This one of Harriet Powers is especially important because it links an appliqué pattern on her apron—a sunburst figure—to images on her masterpiece quilts.

whom she sewed, and she quickly repaid it through her sewing skills.[56] Thus, a black seamstress and her white patrons were linked by the needle, the patrons able to act on their moral convictions and help Keckley, who earned her freedom by sewing.

Creation of the Animals, by Harriet Powers, Athens, Georgia, c. 1886, 105 × 69 inches, appliquéd cottons, with embroidery. M. and M. Karolik Collection, the Museum of Fine Arts, Boston, Massachusetts.

*T*his is one of two surviving quilts made by Harriet Powers, who had been born a slave in 1837. (For a photograph of a detail of the other, see Patsy Orlofsky and Myron Orlofsky, Quilts in America (New York: McGraw-Hill, 1974), p. 306.) These are the only documented nineteenth-century black American quilts with clearly discernible African roots. In their narrative concept, format and technique, they clearly hark back to the traditional appliquéd tapestries of Dahomey in western Africa. Few black American quilts survive from the last century; the story of Harriet Powers' quilts speaks of the fragility of the historical record of women, and especially of black women. As Gladys-Marie Fry (a folklorist who rediscovered and thoroughly researched Powers in the 1970's) tells us, it is an irony and only by chance that these quilts and their remarkable documentation have survived.

Jennie Smith, a white artist and art teacher in Athens, Georgia, saw this quilt exhibited at the Athens Cotton Fair in 1886 and, recognizing its artistic and historic value, tracked down its maker and attempted to buy it. Harriet Powers refused to sell the quilt to Smith at that time, but economics finally forced her to do so in 1890. Had this sale not been made, it is possible that the quilt, like so many others made by poor black women, would have been used up out of necessity and lost to posterity. In a handwritten document which has come down with the quilt, the art teacher tells the story of the exchange:

"Last year I sent word to her that I would buy it if she still wanted to dispose of it. She arrived one afternoon in front of my door in an ox-cart with the precious burden in her lap encased in a clean flour sack. . . . She offered it for ten dollars, but I told her I had only five to give. After going out consulting with her husband she returned and said, 'Owin' to de hardness of de times, my ole man lows I's better teck hit.' Not being a new woman, she obeyed. After giving me a full description of each scene with great earnestness, she departed but has been back several times to visit the darling offspring of her brain. She was only in a measure consoled for its loss when I promised to save her all my scraps." ‹Dr. Gladys-Marie Fry, "Harriet Powers: Portrait of a Black Quilter," in Missing Pieces: Georgia Folk Art 1770–1976 (Atlanta: Georgia Council for the Arts and Humanities, n.d.), pp. 18–19.›

Jennie Smith had the foresight to record Harriet Powers' description of the blocks in Powers' own words, leaving us a firsthand account of the quiltmaker and her vision of the quilt. This single act by an individual has given us a tiny window into what must have been the incredible richness and diversity of the black textile tradition in nineteenth-century America. These two known nineteenth-century examples, by their very existence, sophistication and wholeness, can only begin to suggest what has been lost.

It is clear from the WPA interviews that their sewing and quilting were sources of pride and self-esteem for slave women. They made quilts, one woman recalled, "of many pretty home-made patterns." Another remembered that her mother "used to quilt the prettiest quilts you ever see. . . . Used to sell 'em to de white folks; de best ones Missus hers'f would buy." And in cabins that often contained little furniture beyond beds and stools, always having "plenty of good warm quilts for kiver" was a distinct source of pride.[57] The skills of weaving "stripedy cloth" and of dyeing were also recollected with pleasure. Dye recipes ranged from indigo for blue and madder for red to peach-tree leaves and alum for yellow, walnut stain and copperas for brown to sweet gum bark and copperas for purple. One novel recipe for dyeing, described in the WPA narratives by an ex-slave in Texas, involved burying the cloth in red clay for a week and then soaking it in cold salt water to set.[58]

For slave women as for free white and black women, quiltings, or "sprees," provided sociability and some respite from hard work. There were various kinds of quiltings. The most festive were those that accompanied the corn shuckings regularly held on plantations at harvest time, to which slaves from adjoining plantations or farms were invited. These were "big times" and "grand times" when food, whisky, dancing and singing could be enjoyed after the corn was shucked and the quilts quilted.[59] On large plantations, slaves were sometimes given a holiday at Christmas or New Year's—or, ironically, on the Fourth of July—and the festivities might include a "big time quilting," an all-day event that concluded with an elaborate dinner and dancing. In addition, plantation mistresses often organized smaller quiltings, and slave women organized their own. Especially in winter, when there was less field work to do, women would go from cabin to cabin to help each other make the necessary bedcovers for their families. Such self-initiated gatherings, like the Saturday night "frolics" of their own that slaves might enjoy, could be crucial to the slaves' psychological survival. Historian James Rawick argues that it was through such "non-regimented social relations" that slaves "created and recreated themselves," achieving a sense of community.[60] Given the constant threat to the black family unit under slavery, where members might be sold away, that sense of community was essential. Quilting bees could thus function for black women as they did for white, as invaluable agents of cultural cohesion

It is rare for early southern paintings to portray blacks immersed in their own complex lives and concerns. Most artists chose rather to depict slaves at work, the aspect of their lives which marked them as the property of their owners. The continuity of African cultural traditions in America is dramatically visualized here—in the dance forms, the musical instruments and the headdress. Since we find this cultural persistence in all these forms, and since we know of many twentieth-century black-made quilts which have distinctive African design qualities, we might assume that we are going to find it in nineteenth-century quilts as well. To date, however, only two documented nineteenth-century black American quilts, both by Harriet Powers, have been found which clearly show this link. ▶

and group identity.

The number of authenticated slave-made quilts still extant is extremely small, and we know less, therefore, than we would like about their construction and design motifs. Speculation about the prevalence of strip quilts based on the narrow looms used in West Africa at the time of the slave trade remains speculation, since what strip quilts we in fact have are twentieth-century examples. Research into other aspects of slave culture—their music, their language, their architecture—has revealed strong African roots, and it is possible that the investigations into women's textile work that are currently being undertaken will in time reveal a similar cultural continuity.[61] The existence of such post–Civil War masterpieces as Harriet Powers' Bible quilts, with their demonstrable derivation from Dahomey appliqué techniques, indicates that black women retained a strong sense of their African heritage. Slave women, however, had to function within two conflicting cultural contexts—their own and that of their white masters and mistresses. There is a strong tradition that skilled sewing slaves worked on some of the most elegant southern plantation quilts—a situation that could provoke that "double consciousness," that sense of straddling two worlds, which historians of black culture have described. Nevertheless, it is apparent, as the contemporary black writer Alice Walker has so eloquently said, that slave, and later free, black women could keep their creativity alive through quilts. For a slave woman, a quilt might be "the only medium her position in society allowed her to use"; but it fulfilled her imperative need, that of "ordering the universe in the image of her personal conception of beauty."[62]

The Old Plantation, *unnamed painter, possibly South Carolina, late eighteenth century, 17 7/8 × 11 11/16 inches, watercolor on paper. Collection of Abby Aldrich Rockefeller Folk Art Center, Williamsburg, Virginia.*

*N*ow out of the family, this early quilt came orally documented as being made by a "housemaid and seamstress during slave days." Most slaves, after working all day, returned to their quarters at night to care for their own families. Quilts made by slave women for themselves were by necessity utilitarian— and well used. It would be most unusual for a woman living under the well-documented oppressive conditions of slavery to have made a quilt like this one, with its abundant imported fabric and its meticulous and time-consuming work, for her own use. More likely such a quilt, in very fine condition after a century and a half, was made for the slave holders.

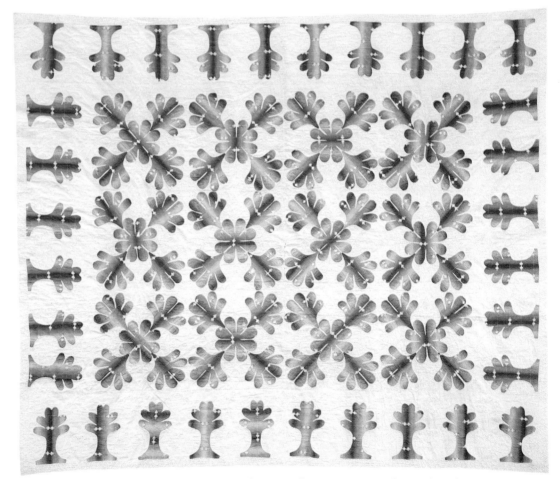

Unknown pattern, c. 1840–1860, southern United States, 93 × 78 inches, appliquéd cottons. Collection of Irma Koski.

O NE OF THE MAJOR and most dramatic developments in the United States throughout the nineteenth century was the expansion of the country westward. From colonial times onward, pioneers had pushed into the continent's interior from their eastern seaboard settlements, first crossing the Appalachian range and reaching to the Mississippi River. The nineteenth century itself would see a succession of new frontiers, as settlers moved across the Mississippi to the Missouri River, then leapt across the prairie and the great plains to the Pacific Coast, and finally, in the post–Civil War years, penetrated into and settled the trans-Missouri west of Nebraska and the Dakotas. Aware that they were participating in a major historical event, women left more records of their pioneering experience than of any other event except the Civil War. The essential role that women played at every stage in the experience of migration and settlement might also be told through their quilts. Quilts accompanied them on the western journey, were made on the journey, were instruments of both physical and psychological survival on new frontiers, and became both emblems and agents of that domestic world which women saw it as their responsibility to recreate in their new homes.

Preparations for the westward journey, especially if it were to cover the thousands of miles of mountain and desert to the Pacific coast, might begin months before. In addition to the food staples that had to be packed—hundreds of pounds of dried fruit, flour, corn meal, sugar and rice—women had to plan carefully the clothing and bedding to be taken. Keturah Belknap was already a seasoned emigrant when she and her husband decided to leave for Oregon in 1848; following a classic migration pattern, she had already moved from Ohio to Indiana to Illinois and thence across the Mississippi to Iowa. With careful planning, she nonetheless spent over six months sewing in preparation for the trip to Oregon—jeans and shirts ("clothes enough to last a year"), six two-bushel bags or sacks, for which she first spun the thread, to trans-

port the food supplies, and a formidable cover of two thicknesses, linen and muslin, for the wagon. Mrs. Mary E. Hampton, leaving North Carolina for Texas, recorded taking "all my feather-beds and quilts," and Sue Sanders, newly married at fifteen and also emigrating to Texas, commented that the first supplies her mother packed for her in the wagon were a feather bed, two pillows, bedding and quilts. To these, she said, she added "quilts of my own . . . for I had always prided myself on the way I could piece and quilt them." [63]

Warm covering would be essential in the imperfectly chinked log cabins or the dirt and mud sod houses the emigrants would construct at journey's end and, for those without sufficient covering, the

Vintage photograph of pioneers on one of the overland trails, c. 1850–1880.
Collection of the Denver Public Library, Western History Department (negative number F12921), Colorado.

P̶ioneers moving westward, conscious that they were making an epic journey, left us a great deal of material about their lives: we have their pictures, their words and their possessions. Photographers also made the journey, to record the land, equipment, architecture—and faces. Looking directly at us, this group must have known that at least in their own lives there would be no more monumental episode. This image makes vivid the fatigue and emotional strain of the harrowing journey undertaken by whole families, including children and infants.

Women left numerous journals—and, of course, their quilts. Quilts were made to be used on the trip for warmth and protection, or as packing or, all too often, as burying cloths. Some were made in anticipation of the arrival at new "homes," often in the middle of nowhere. Some quilts served as memory—a woman's own first quilt, a brother's crib quilt, a wedding quilt made by her mother. And a great many women carried quilts composed of blocks signed by friends and family with precious messages from those left behind, whom they would likely never see again.

*I*n carrying quilts, and especially friendship ones,
on the overland trails, women could, in a sense,
bring their loved ones with them. The staggering
numbers of such quilts made during the height of
the migrations to places like Ohio, Indiana, Illinois, Minnesota, Wisconsin, the Plains states, Oregon and California in the 1840's and 1850's, and
the care with which so many of them have been
handed down, speak of their deeply felt value. They
helped pioneers transcend the anguish and heal the
pain of lifelong separations.

*I*n 1853, Hannah Williams and her husband
Thomas left Joplin, Missouri, to cross the continent on the Oregon Trail. They were part of a train
which very nearly did not make it, arriving in late
October. Years later, she used her needle to memori-
alize that historic voyage. She stitched their photographs (tintypes) to a small section of the canvas
that covered their wagon, with an affectionate
embroidered message about the "old tent." Here,
we are looking at textiles as text, "reading" a
nineteenth-century textile for a deeper and more
intimate understanding of what life was like for
ordinary Americans. Hannah Williams has truly
left us a "page" of that history.

weeks preceding departure might see a flurry of quilt
activity. Miriam Davis Colt's friends held two bees for
her prior to her departure from New York state for
Kansas in 1856. One was for the elderly ladies, one for
the younger, and both, she recorded in her diary,
"united pleasure with business." [64] Such sewing and
quilting bees often served as ceremonial leave-takings.
Women might be seeing friends and kin for the last
time, severing ties with a female world inside which
they had lived all their lives. Scholars agree that for
women the westward movement could be a major dis-
location. It was husbands and fathers who, catching
the "western fever," decided to emigrate; often the
women were not consulted, and they went reluc-
tantly, even "with anguish." [65] The friendship quilts
that were made for women moving west are in this
context especially significant. It is no accident that
their greatest vogue was in the 1840's and 1850's, decades of great social mobility and of major migrations
via the overland trails to California and Oregon. With
their inscribed signatures, loving messages and blocks
incorporating bits of the clothing of their makers, the
friendship quilts were visible and tactile reminders
of connectedness, protests against the severance of

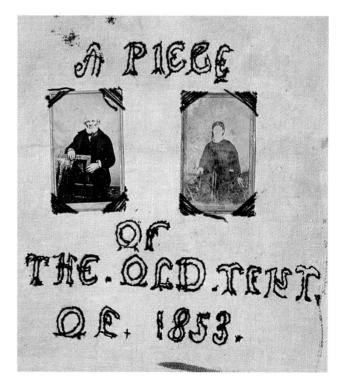

*"A PIECE OF THE OLD TENT OF 1853,"
by Hannah Williams, Oregon, date unknown.
Collection of the Lane County Historical Museum, Eugene, Oregon.*

Map of Kansas, by H. A. Deuel, Kansas, 1887, 86 1/2 × 69 1/2 inches, pieced and embroidered wools.
Collection of the Kansas State Historical Society / Kansas Museum of History, Topeka.

Crazy quilts, made from random (not repeated) shapes, are sometimes said to resemble landscapes or maps. This unusual quilt is a map. The quiltmaker used what she knew—the traditional materials, forms and techniques of the popular crazy quilt—to make a proud statement of Kansas statehood (1861). Embroidery stitches mark significant details: county lines, county names and, most importantly, the rivers which served as veins of life to the farmers. Quilts are bordered; so are states, this one by Nebraska, Missouri, Colorado and the Indian Territory (in 1907 to become Oklahoma).

ties but at the same time affirmations that physical distance would not destroy emotional bonds.[66]

Friendship and other precious quilts were taken on the journey even when space in the heavily packed wagons had to be measured carefully. Sarah Cummins, leaving for Oregon in 1845, carefully selected among her most valuable possessions "my little chair of Sugar Maple wood," books, "many rare bits of needlework" and "my stock of spare quilts" made from costly Revolutionary War calicoes.[67] The quilts that accompanied women moving west and that they so carefully preserved could themselves tell the story of the migration patterns of the nineteenth century. Even a partial listing of the quilts currently housed in the Nebraska Historical Society, for example, suggests the great social mobility, the distances traversed by pioneering men and women. There is a pre–Civil War *Log Cabin* quilt from South Carolina, a silk *Log Cabin* from Pennsylvania, a star quilt from Vermont, an appliqué with trapunto quilting from New York state, a magnificent 1858 appliqué bride's quilt from Baltimore that arrived in one of Nebraska's earliest settlements, a *Flying Geese* quilt made in Maryland in 1779, and a whole-cloth quilt of linen and wool made in New York state in 1796. Others arrived in Nebraska, in patterns from *Melon Patch* to *Lone Star* to *Sunburst*, to *Eight-Pointed Star*, *Dove in the Window* and *Crazy* from Ohio, Illinois, Indiana and Missouri. Elsewhere, a quilt might traverse the better part of the continent, as did a blue-and-white cotton quilt made in Vermont in 1809 that accompanied its maker and her descendants to New York, and then to Ohio and Indiana, finally arriving in Minnesota in 1887.[68]

On the journey itself quilts did heroic service. Thick comforts and quilts were used to line wagons, making them, as one woman wrote, "impervious to wind and weather."[69] They were wrapped around fragile china, used to pad and soften the wagon seats and to protect the exposed sides of wagons during Indian attacks. And they were used to bury the dead.

The stories of nineteenth-century quilts are most often physically separated from them. If we have information at all, it usually comes through oral history, from the family or from diaries. Rarely do we find a quilt like this one, with a great deal of information written upon the cloth. In an era when illness and death were one's intimate companions (in 1827, in New York, nearly half of all children died before the age of five), quilts could serve as lasting memorials to the living and to the dead.

Detail of Le Moyne Star quilt top, 1859, origin unknown, pieced cottons. Collection of Al and Merry Silber.

Mortality on the westward journey was high. One historian says of the long overland trip to the Pacific coast that "there is scarcely a diary written during the 1840's which does not record the death of a father or husband or child or wife along the way."[70] In the treeless stretches of the plains and desert, where no wood was available, or simply because of a wagon train's need not to pause or delay, quilts were used

There were twenty thousand deaths on the Oregon Trail; one out of every seventeen pioneers was lost en route. It is estimated that there was an average of one grave every eighty yards between the Missouri River and the Willamette Valley, Oregon. "Along some stretches of the route graves were so numerous that the trail developed a saw-tooth edge — a border of footpaths worn by the curious going off to the side to read the wooden grave markers." ‹Huston Horn, The Old West: The Pioneers (New York: Time-Life Books, 1974), p. 97.›

instead of coffins to bury the dead. The diary of a woman in 1849 described the burial of a mother and infant: "The bodies were wrapped together in a bed comforter and wound, quite mummified with a few yards of string that we made by tying together torn strips of a cotton dress shirt."[71]

It was the women who were more preoccupied with death on the journey—one woman counted and recorded in her diary the graves passed each day. They were concerned with maintaining family ties, family stability, and they took seriously their sphere role as moral and cultural agents. Sewing was a reassurance of their civilized female identity. They packed work baskets with sewing for spare moments, carried their "bags of pieces," as Miriam Davis Colt did, and they visited from wagon to wagon, where "tatting, knitting, crocheting" and exchanging food recipes "kept us in practice of feminine occupations."[72] They made quilt blocks and quilts. While crossing the plains by wagon train in 1859, Sarah Elliott Morse made a flower-basket quilt that contains the names of the women and some of the men in the party.[73]

A snapshot of spring cleaning gives us a good look at what must have been the entire inventory of the bedding in a cabin near Seattle around 1890. There are tied comforts, pieced quilts, woven coverlets and some crocheted pillow tops. The woman has chosen a day without rain to air her bedding. Quilts, made after arrival or carried along on overland journeys, warmed a home: "The gay colored quilts which came across in a big chest, and which had been used as wrapping for a few cherished dishes and other treasures, were unpacked.... Other bits from the old home three thousand miles away were placed on the crude shelves: a picture of grandmother's parents; a few books; the family Bible; the little treasures which had slipped between the bedding in an old chest and a queer looking trunk lined with bright flowered paper. They were now at home." ‹ Leonore Gale Barette, Christmas in Oregon Territory in 1853, (1950), pp. 5–6, quoted in Glenn Mason, "A Piece of the Old Tent" (Eugene, Ore.: Lane County Pioneer Museum, 1976), p. 27. ›

Vintage photograph of woman airing quilts outside her cabin in Green Lake, Seattle, Washington, c. 1890. Special Collections Division, University of Washington Libraries (negative number UW 593), Seattle.

An 1886 photograph of the Reeder family, near Merna, Nebraska, by Solomon Butcher. Solomon D. Butcher Collection/Nebraska State Historical Society, Lincoln.

"*The sod house usually reflected the austerity of the scenery and life of the plains. The houses were severe and unadorned. Except for the natural embroidery of prairie flowers growing in the yard and on the soddy roof, there was little decoration that was not functional. Mrs. Clarence Carr recalled of her Dawson County sod house, 'My mother was always throwing flower seed up on our roof; they would bloom out in damp weather.'*
‹*Roger L. Welsch*, Sod Walls: The Story of the Nebraska Sod House *(Broken Bow, Nebr.: Purcells, Inc., 1968), p. 88.* ›

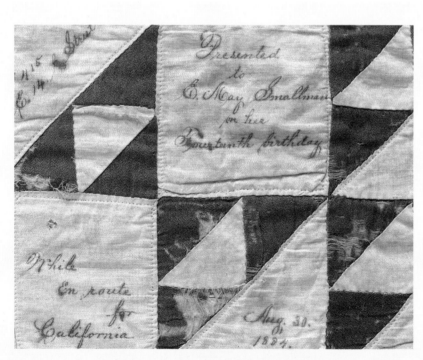

Detail of unknown pattern quilt (called "Road to California" by the family), by members of the Hezlep and Shuey families, Illinois to California, 1858–1859, pieced cottons, with ink inscriptions. Collection of Ellen Reasoner Lopez.

Here is one small section of an extraordinary record, a quilt which literally tells the story of a family's journey from Illinois to California. Other blocks say: "Piec(e)s cut in the winter of 1858," "Left Illinois for California—April 15th, 1859," "Crossed the Plains," "Arrived in Columbia, California on October 28, 1859," "Seven months on the road" and an enthusiastic "Ho for California!" The inscription shown here reveals that the precious quilt was given to a young family member years later to celebrate her birthday.

Upon arriving at their destinations, women used their quilts both as protection against cold weather and as decoration in the primitive shelters. The use of quilts to cover door and window openings was widespread. One woman remembered the nightly ritual in her Minnesota home in the late nineteenth century, when her father would "cut the kindling with a draw-knife, hang up the quilt at the outer door, throw down the old coat at the sill, bank the fire, and declare it bed time."[74] And the yearning to turn the first rudely and hastily built shelter into a "home" led women to ingenious uses: a side table was made from an old barrel covered with a piece of patchwork in an 1840 Illinois log cabin; a board supported by chairs and "covered with folded quilts" became an "impromptu sofa" for a wedding; a folded quilt placed in the deep window embrasure of a sod hut created a sunny space for children to play and a mother to sew. Hanging quilts on the dirt walls of sod huts or the unboarded parts of a log cabin "made them seem homelike," as one woman said. And when Lucy Larcom's sister hung up a "patch curtain" in her pioneer Illinois home, Larcom was poetically reminded of "the days of ancient tapestried halls."[75]

The need for beauty and for color, as a way of civilizing the frontier but also, often, for psychic survival in isolated areas where neighbors were far distant, could be intense. A Wisconsin woman in 1863 rode twenty miles on horseback to obtain a certain calico for a peony appliqué quilt; Grace Snyder's mother, living in a Nebraska homestead of "two naked little soddies squatting on a bare, windswept ridge above a narrow, winding canyon," took flour sacks, bleached them, and embroidered them in flying red birds to create curtains for the sod-house windows.[76] One wonders if the red were turkey red, that most popular of quilt colors during one hundred years of American quiltmaking. The woman who wrote to *The Woman's Magazine* in 1889 about turkey red spoke for countless others who, like her, had found the color a special beneficence. Its purity, brightness, durability and "cheapness in the purchase," the writer proclaimed, made turkey red "'a thing of beauty and a joy forever.'" Her list of the ways in which it could be used included "in a baby dress, a child's pinafore, a doll's frock, mother's apron, father's pocket handkerchief, a curtain, cushion, tablecloth," as well as "a lambrequin for shelf or corner bracket...a boy's necktie, a hat brimming...an occasional extra dress," and of course "a bedquilt." That the color was, she

This image, with three young women hamming for the camera and playing at housework, belies the reality of the staggering amount and varieties of work required of most nineteenth-century women to maintain the home. Throughout the century, entries in women's diaries and work journals read like litanies, listing the endless repetitive tasks, including: soap making, carding, spinning, weaving, dyeing, washing, ironing, gardening, butchering, smoking and salting meats, canning, cooking, shearing and plucking, tending animals, child rearing and nursing the old and the sick. Sewing was paramount. For most women, bedcoverings, sheets, pillows, towels, window coverings as well as clothing for every member of the family had to be made from scratch—and these articles wore out and had to be replaced.

Except for the diary and journal entries, nothing remains of most of the grueling labor. But of the few remaining housework artifacts made by women, it is most often the quilts that have been carefully saved and remain as testaments to the remarkable industry and creativity of nineteenth-century women.

*Vintage photograph of women doing housework, Eureka, California, c. 1910.
Collection of Peter Palmquist, Arcata, California.*

concluded, refreshing not just to the eye but "through the eye to the inner sense" suggests that strong need for psychological and spiritual sustenance voiced by many pioneer women which they satisfied through home decoration and particularly through the making of quilts.[77]

Ideally that quiltmaking became a co-operative endeavor, as soon as neighbors were available. Historians of the West have emphasized how important it was for women to create female support systems, co-operative networks in newly settled areas. Women suffered more than men from the settlement patterns that characterized the West—far-flung farms or homesteads miles distant from the nearest neighbors and from towns. Men had more mobility, making trips for supplies or to trade, and were often absent for weeks at a time, working at other jobs. With their former female world ruptured, women had to create a new one: it was part of creating an environment, that domestic-cultural space within which they existed. The nineteenth-century doctrine of separate spheres meant that women lived "a large portion of their

Nature, with its cycles of death and renewal, provided a wellspring for women who needed models for both physical and psychological survival. Lush gardens sprang forth on beds, even when the land was not yet accommodating. The flowers and leaves on most quilts are highly stylized, but some, like those on this quilt, testify to the closeness with which women observed life around them.

Garden, c. 1850–1860, Ohio, 90 × 91 inches, appliquéd cottons. Courtesy of America Hurrah Antiques, New York City.

58

Less than a decade after some pioneers walked across the continent, the transcontinental railroad was completed (1869), bringing changes never before imaginable. Travel, communication and goods became available to areas once remote and isolated; the country was suddenly a much smaller place. A profound transformation was taking place, and perhaps this is what Mrs. Saunders was commenting upon in her quilt top. In 1884 the Canton-Aberdeen-Nashville Railroad (which was to become the Illinois Central) first went through the town of Kosciusko in Mississippi. It is believed that it was then that Mrs. Saunders fashioned her inventive work.

Train quilt top, probably made by Mrs. Saunders, Kosciusko, Mississippi, c. 1884, 90¼ × 101 inches, pieced and appliquéd cottons, with embroidery. Collection of the State Historical Museum, Mississippi Department of Archives and History, Jackson.

emotional life well within a wholly female affectional circle." They depended upon each other for physical, psychological and emotional support. In the 1870's, when Luna Kellie arrived in Nebraska, there was "not a tree a shrub not even a gooseberry bush." Eventually she found a woman who became her friend: "Without that friendship that day begun I know I must have fainted and dropped by the way ere many years had flown." The autobiographies and memoirs of women who lived through the pioneer experience again and again describe the importance to them of such female friendships. In 1853, Rebecca H. N. Woodson was eighteen years old, newly married, and newly arrived in Sonoma City, California. In an autobiographical sketch she wrote in later years, she recalled meeting some neighboring women: "It was a great comfort to me as I soon got acquainted with them and many many happy hours have I spent in their company.... There was scarcely ever a day we was not togeather [sic]. We did not think we could start to make a new dress or start piecing a new quilt without consulting each other." A woman describing the early days of pioneer life in the Western Reserve in Ohio remembered "how they quilted in companies," and another, who settled in Texas in the 1830's, recalled the "quiltin' bees" where, although the

"*I* went to Mrs. Low's quilting. There was 15 to quilt had 2 quilts and there was indeed many meery faces about them," reported one young Iowa pioneer. "This afternoon," wrote Elisabeth Adams, "I go to Sewing Society at Mr. Pierces. I suppose the affairs of town will be discussed over the quilt." ‹ *Julie Roy Jeffrey,* Frontier Women *(New York: Hill and Wang, 1979), p. 86.* ›

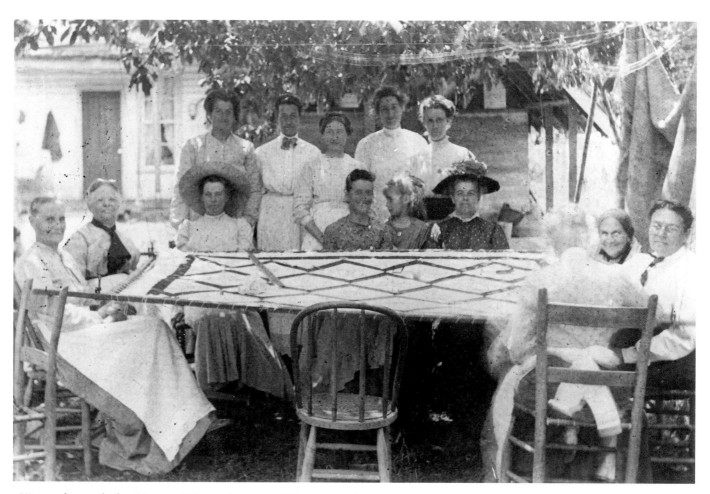

Vintage photograph of quilting bee, Mehama, Oregon, c. 1905. Courtesy of the Oregon Historical Society (negative number ORHI 21876), Portland.

women might try "to out-rival each other in the daintiness of their stitches...they helped each other in every way.... They helped each other. Perhaps this thought justifies the whole of pioneer woman's suffering."[78]

After the first arduous years of pioneering, as population increased and towns developed, sewing and quilting continued to knot women together through bees, societies and fairs. Needlework skills remained a primary form of bonding, and those without such skills might have "little access to the major institution of women's social life." A Swedish woman who emigrated to Kansas in the early 1850's found that being invited to sewings and quiltings was a sign of friendship and acceptance. Her pleasure in receiving these invitations was such that she recalled in her autobiog-

*I*n nineteenth-century rural America, social rituals grew up around tasks which could be accomplished quickly and efficiently by many hands. With the help of lots of friends and neighbors, a man could raise a small barn in one long day of work. Women had their equivalent in the quilting bee, where several women got together for the day to do the tedious, time-consuming work of finishing a quilt top made by one of them. Working together, they stitched through the three layers and added the finishing touches. Sometimes, these quiltings were held simultaneously with the barn raisings, with a grand joyous feast ending the day of hard work and great pride. "The finishing of this quilt made a gala day for the neighborhood. It was unrolled and cut out with much excitement.... It was truly a beautiful thing, ... an expression of the life of its occupants, a fit covering for those who made it." ‹Ellen H. Rollings, New England Bygones (Philadelphia: Lippincott, 1883), p. 238.›

Vintage photograph of a barn raising, Vermont, c. 1900. Collection of the Vermont Historical Society (negative number ATX 255), Montpelier.

Crazy, by "The Ladies of the Christian Church," Centralia, Illinois, 1892, silks, velvets and taffetas.
Techniques include embroidery and paint work. Private collection.

Working in the classic Victorian crazy-quilt style so popular at the time, the women of the Christian Church of Centralia, Illinois, apparently organized a quilt to represent their town at the gigantic World's Columbian Exposition held in Chicago's Jackson Park in 1893. The quilt is, in fact, a rare graphic depiction of a town at the turn of the century, a kind of city directory, with Centralia's four (!) newspapers at its center, the town's businesses, individuals and families filling in the rest of the quilt's surface.

Detail of Vine, by Susan McCord, McCordsville, Indiana, c. 1860–1880, pieced and appliquéd cottons. Collection of the Henry Ford Museum & Greenfield Village, Dearborn, Michigan.

The wilderness and the dry land shall be glad,
The desert shall rejoice and blossom;
Like the crocus it shall blossom abundantly,
And rejoice with joy and singing.
Isaiah 35 :1

raphy inviting the women in return to an all-day quilting at her home, at which she served the best dinner she could prepare—chicken and wild-grape pie. A visitor to Topeka, Kansas, in the 1850's attended meetings of both the temperance society and the sewing circle and remarked that although "the ladies [came] from almost all states in the Union," they "seemed to be bound together in strong bonds of friendship." Sewing thus was often the common denominator through which women who were strangers to each other could bridge the distances between them. Women who might otherwise have little in common could always discuss "their patchwork an' knittin'," as a character in one of Zona Gale's novels of Iowa observed.[79]

In addition to quiltings and sewing bees, agricultural fairs in settled regions enabled women to participate in and enjoy the fruits of their common culture. Quilt exhibits, competitions and prizes seem to have been features of town, county and state fairs from the very first one in Pittsfield, Massachusetts, in 1808. Long after the United States had embarked on industrialization, agricultural fairs continued to be

associated in the popular mind with exemplary domestic and rural virtues. After the War of 1812, with the nation eager to establish its independence of imported English and European goods, fairs, or the household manufactures displayed at them, came to represent, in the words of the *Niles Register,* "all the virtues—moral, religious and political."[80] Homegrown and homemade products were symbols of the Jeffersonian ideal of a sturdy, self-reliant agricultural population as the source and guarantee of democratic values. Fairs flourished in rural areas throughout the nineteenth century, and families looked forward to them eagerly as holiday occasions. A Pennsylvania woman remembered her excitement as a child in the 1870's getting ready for the fair, as her mother hurried to finish a special piece of needlework to be displayed. A young girl noted in her diary in 1853 that at the fair "Pa took three premiums for grapes, Ma, two for flowers, and bed quilt, and I, two for flowers and painting."[81] As opportunities to exhibit quilts, compare workmanship, look for new ideas, find (and sometimes even purchase) new quilt patterns, fairs were a consistent stimulus to women's quilt culture, and an exhibited quilt could be the source of both personal and civic pride.

Susan McCord no doubt exhibited many of her magnificent quilts at local and county fairs, and both her quilts and her life contain features that make them exemplary of that phase of nineteenth-century life—after the first arduous years of pioneer settlement and before the growth of congested cities—that came to represent in the popular mind an "ideal" America. McCord was an Indiana farm woman whose eighty-year-long life spanned most of the century. A mother and homemaker who in the early years of her marriage lived in a log cabin, she made butter and soap, gardened and preserved, was an herbalist, neighborhood doctor and midwife. As a member of the Methodist church, she belonged to what was by mid-century the largest Protestant denomination in the country (and one intimately associated with quilt-making, from Baltimore album quilts through the woman's temperance movement). Her quilts—scrap quilts and elegant appliqué, in patterns ranging from a *Grandmother's Flower Garden* to a *Turkey Tracks* to crazy quilts—cover the spectrum of American quilt-making.[82] At least three of the thirteen of her quilts that survive are variations on the theme of the garden, and *Vine,* her greatest quilt, draws upon similar iconography and associations. If pioneer men were popularly seen as subduing or conquering the wilderness, women saw their mission, as scholars have been recently demonstrating, as that of cultivating that wilderness, making of it a "domestic Eden."[83] Both western promotional literature and fiction and the imperatives of the cult of domesticity encouraged women "to claim the new frontier as a garden of their own," to fulfill the Biblical injunctions, with which they were all deeply familiar, to "make the wilderness rejoice and blossom as the rose" and to "cultivate one's vineyard." A garden is a way of domesticating the wild, of creating an ordered and patterned space whose bounty is the result of shared natural and human effort. So many of women's quilts are metaphorical gardens, suggesting both in their designs and in the processes of their making a way of experiencing, of looking at and responding to life. McCord's *Vine,* with its harmonious composition of curving vertical strips from which depend exquisitely pieced leaves, is a visual testament to an orderly and abundant landscape. And composed as it is of the scraps left from her children's and grandchildren's clothing, the quilt is testament as well to those qualities of

joining and connecting, of creating out of fragments harmonious wholes, that represented in the nineteenth century women's highest domestic function and that are today the source of so much of the fascination of quilts. For a contemporary painter turned quilter like Joyce Parr, for instance, the joining or re-membering process of quilting is itself "redemptive," a healing activity. Integrating textiles, a woman integrates herself, and her world.[84]

*I*n their traditional names and sometimes in their construction, nineteenth-century quilts reflect what women saw around them and what was important in their lives. Here, we seem to be looking down into a series of log-cabin houses, each with the traditional red hearth at the center. Dolores Hayden and Peter Marris, in "The Quiltmaker's Landscape," talk about quiltmakers as the real and metaphorical architects of their spaces: "Quilt blocks . . . reflected women's familiarity with the tools of frontier settlement—especially building tools. After an American woman, Tabitha Babbitt, invented the circular saw, the block named Circular Saw developed. Women also pieced Monkey Wrench and Double Monkey Wrench, as well as Carpenter's Square, Saw Tooth, Compass, and Anvil patterns. Women knew how to use these tools, as well as the familiar household implements whose designs are depicted in the Churn Dash and Pickle Dish blocks." "Because women often made use of their knowledge of carpentry, building design, and urban structure when they designed quilts, we need the pictorial conventions of architecture and landscape architecture, as well as the conventions of needlework, to decipher their meanings." ‹Dolores Hayden and Peter Marris, "The Quiltmaker's Landscape," Landscape, XXV, 3 (1981), pp. 45, 40.›*

Log Cabin, c. 1870–1890, origin unknown, 68 × 78 inches, silks and wools. Collection of The Fine Arts Museums of San Francisco, gift of Mrs. M. Gannon.

I N THE COURSE of the nineteenth century, American women compiled for themselves an extensive record of participation in a broad spectrum of benevolent and social reform movements. Contemporary studies are documenting the scope of this activity—from church-related charitable and missionary work to abolition to Civil War relief to temperance and suffrage—emphasizing its importance, often, in helping to create significant social change and in enabling women to re-define and enlarge their sphere, to "reshape the boundaries of public and private space."[85] None of the studies, however, recognizes the major role that women's sewing played in their reform activity: how they used their needles as weapons in their campaigns against a variety of social ills and injustices. A history of women's reform work as told through their sewing shows them using it to raise money, to garner public attention and support, and thereby to claim for themselves a more visible and active public and political role.

According to contemporary historians, sewing for charitable and benevolent purposes probably arrived with the first colonists, and by the beginning of the nineteenth century every large city and town had societies that supplied soup, sewing and firewood to the poor. The years from 1800 to 1830 saw a great expansion of organized benevolent work, and it was women who were identified with virtually all public welfare activities. Sarah Josepha Hale, for example, was a pioneer reformer. In 1833 she founded the Seaman's Aid Society, which provided not charity but work to help enable the indigent wives and widows of Boston sailors to become self-supporting. In Utica, New York, between 1830 and 1860, according to historian Mary Ryan, women's public-welfare work, which included establishing and running orphan asylums and "ragged schools" for poor children in addition to their charity sewing, probably surpassed in economic value the city's official annual monetary appropriation for the poor.[86]

Most of this benevolent work was church-affiliated. In the nineteenth century, women were the church-goers; no other institution so cultivated their loyalty, and no other institution allowed them even the limited scope that the churches did for exercising their powers. Every Protestant church had its Sewing Society or Female Prayer Meeting, its Women's Guild or Fancy Work Improvement Club. Ladies Aid, Priscilla and Dorcas Societies, and African Dorcas Societies in black churches, were established in every town, city or newly settled territory almost as soon as the churches themselves. Women held fairs, festivals and bazaars at which they sold their needlework products, baked goods and preserves in order to raise money for charity, for the financial needs of the churches themselves—including everything from new pews or a new organ to paying part of the minister's salary—and for the domestic and foreign missions.

The missionary movement was a major Protestant enterprise throughout the century, and women's participation and support were extensive. In the pre–Civil War period, when missions were established in western states and territories to Christianize the American Indians, women supplied funds and barrels and boxes of clothing and bedding that they shipped to mission stations. In 1846, Harriette Kidder described in her diary a church meeting at which over two hundred dollars was raised for the missionary cause, and two fund-raising quilts with signatures at twenty-five cents each were presented to the missionaries.[87] The ten-cent fund-raising quilt was ubiquitous. As late as 1910, a Methodist woman's group in Normal, Illinois, was using one to raise money for missionary work. Children—boys as well as girls—were often organized into their own charitable societies, called, for example, the Sunbeams, the Young People's Society of Christian Endeavor, the Young Helpers and the Little Workers. Often they would piece and make quilts, "voting, when complete, whether the home hospital, or the half-frozen Alaska Mission, is to receive them."[88] In 1881, Henrietta Jones of Watertown, New York, described finishing "a patchwork quilt for Willie [her son] to put in the missionary box. He had done much of the sewing himself."[89]

The association of sewing with Christian concep-

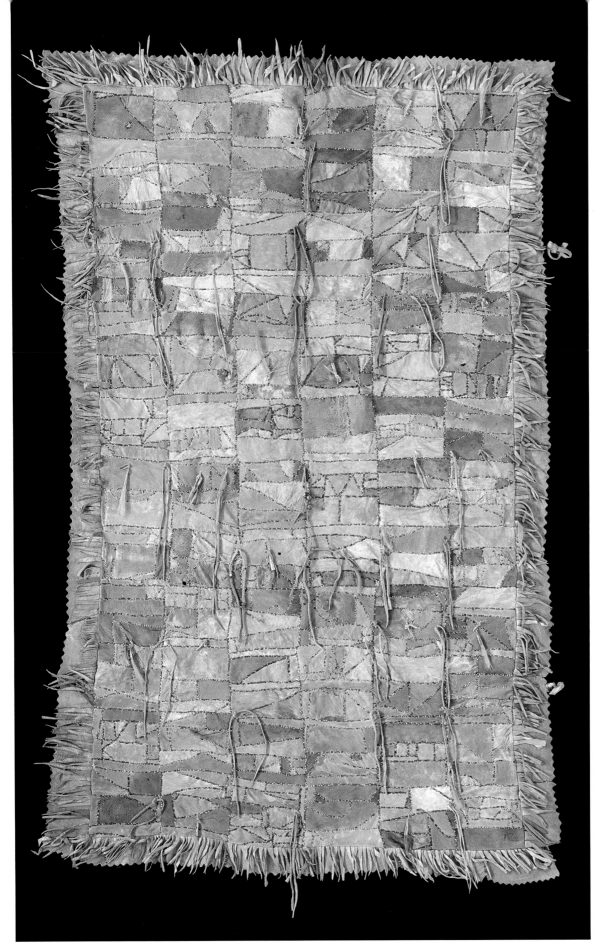

*U*sing traditional
Sioux material
(hides) and the tradi-
tional size and shape of
a pony blanket, this In-
dian needlewoman em-
ployed the new fashion
of a crazy quilt, incor-
porating trade beads.
The result is a unique,
skillful and complex
blending of Sioux and
Victorian traditions.

Crazy, by a Sioux needlewoman, South Dakota, c. 1880–1900, 41 × 64 inches,
beaded suede, with fringe. Collection of the Roger J. Bounds Foundation, Inc.

Vintage photograph of Sioux, Sioux camp, Hot Springs, South Dakota, c. 1900.
Collection of Sandra Mitchell.

tions of industry and virtue and with proper womanly behavior carried over into the actual work of the missionaries, who taught sewing and quilting to newly converted Indian women. British author and social critic Frances Trollope, attending an exhibit of Indian craft work in Washington, D.C., in 1827, singled out the "specimens of worked muslin, and other needle-work . . . all proving clearly that [Indians] are perfectly capable of civilization"; and a woman missionary in Oregon wrote approvingly of the missionaries' success in realigning sex roles according to white cultural models: "When an Indian woman ceases to do a man's work, she learns the household arts. It is an interesting sight to see her seated on the ground with a child on each side whom she is teaching to sew." [90]

Fortunately, not all white observers of Indian life assumed such attitudes of cultural superiority. Helen Doyle, traveling in the Sierras, was enchanted by the beauty of Indian women's basket work, and it was her knowledge of quilting, rooted in her childhood, that enabled her to appreciate their craftsmanship and artistry. The intricately patterned baskets, woven of maidenhair fern and redbud bark and hand-dyed, recalled for her "the quilting patterns that Mama had

done so beautifully. It seemed to me these Indian women traded with each other for the materials for their treasure baskets much as the women in northern New York exchanged pieces for their quilts. They exhibited them with the same sense of pride that the New England women did their handiwork." [91] Eventually, of course, Indian women developed their own quilt designs and traditions, and American quiltmaking as a whole was vastly enriched by the mutual exchange between whites and Indians of ideas and patterns. Quilt pattern names like *Indian Hatchet* and *Indian Trail* attest to the influence of Indian culture on white quilting. And if missionaries sought to Christianize through quilting, the groups among whom they proselytized often ingeniously adapted the white artifact to their own cultural purposes. Northern Plains Indian men used quilts as blankets in rites of fasting and prayer; and quilts were major items in the "give-aways," or ceremonial re-distributions of wealth among Plains Indians. [92] Hawaiian women, introduced to quilting by Methodist missionaries in 1820, not only raised folding and cutting techniques to new levels of sophistication and developed their own distinctive symbolic designs; they also utilized the quilt form, which had been a colonial imposition, to assert their own nationalism, creating the Royal Hawaiian Flag quilt as a proud expression of their own cultural identity and political sentiments.[93]

USING QUILTS and quilt designs to make political statements was of course also a practice of American needleworkers, and the anti-slavery movement, which from the 1830's to the eve of the Civil War would enlist the sewing skills of large numbers of north-ern women, was reflected in many quilt patterns. *Underground Railroad,* with its series of contrasting light and dark squares leading to central areas sug-gesting the "safe houses" that harbored escaping slaves along the route to Canada, was a powerful visual dramatization of the checkered and dangerous path to freedom. And as early as 1825 the renaming of the *Job's Tears* pattern as *Slave Chain* indicated north-ern women's political sentiments.[94] These sentiments became mobilized with the establishment of the first Female Anti-Slavery Societies, including both black

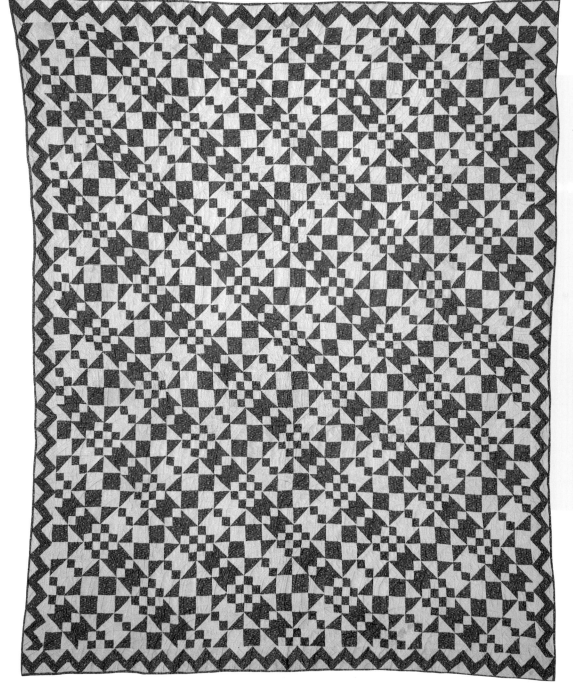

Beginning in the 1830's, slavery was an issue discussed and passionately debated throughout the country; it seemed to have had a special resonance for women. The naming and renaming of quilt designs was a way for ordinary women to ex-press their concerns and ideas. Patterns which had for years had Bibli-cal or domestic refer-ences were given new, more relevant names by women who had current social concerns on their minds. This quilt pat-tern, which had been known as Jacob's Lad-der, came to be called, by many women, Underground Railroad.

Underground Railroad, c. 1870–1890, probably Kentucky, 72 1/2 × 87 inches, pieced cottons.
Collection of Richard and Suellen Meyer.

On the left we see Harriet Tubman (1823–1913) with seven of the three hundred or more slaves she rescued when she was a conductor on the Underground Railroad. These were perilous journeys; escaping slaves risked imprisonment, torture and death. An account of one of the nineteen escapes Tubman engineered and led between 1845 and 1855 makes vivid how harrowing and dangerous they were: "Auburn, Dec. 30, 1860 . . . We have been expending our sympathies, as well as congratulations, on seven newly arrived slaves that Harriet Tubman has just pioneered safely from the Southern Part of Maryland. —One woman carried a baby all the way and bro't two other chld'n that Harriet and the men helped along. They bro't a piece of old comfort and a blanket, in a basket with a little kindling, a little bread for the baby with some laudanum to keep it from crying during the day. They walked all night carrying the little ones, and spread the old comfort on the frozen ground, in some dense thicket where they all hid, while Harriet went out foraging, and sometimes cd not get back till dark, fearing she wd be followed. Then, if they had crept further in, and she couldn't find them, she wd whistle, or sing certain hymns and they wd answer." ‹Martha C. Wright to Ellen Wright, William Lloyd Garrison Manuscripts, Sophia Smith Collection, Smith College, Northampton, Massachusetts, quoted in Black Women in White America, *ed. by Gerda Lerner (New York: Vintage Books, 1972), pp. 64–65.›*

"Deliver me from the oppression of man." The image of the bound slave was incorporated into a wide range of popular commercial items, ranging from china dishes (Josiah Wedgwood was a dedicated English abolitionist) to penwipes and needle cases.

Detail of quilt on page 71.

Vintage photograph of Harriet Tubman and runaway slaves, date unknown.
Sophia Smith Collection, Smith College, Northampton, Massachusetts.

Unknown pattern, by Deborah Coates, Lancaster County, Pennsylvania, c. 1840–1850, 96½ × 89 inches, pieced silks, with stamp work. Collection of Marjorie A. Laidman.

*T*he Coates family of Lancaster County, Pennsylvania was well-known in the early part of the nineteenth century. Lindley Coates was documented by traditional history as he was a prominent and active abolitionist, a Quaker who was among the organizers of the Anti-Slavery Society (1833) and who preceded William Lloyd Garrison as president of the American Anti-Slavery Association in 1840. What we know of Coates's wife's role and her abolitionist sentiments has been recorded in a very subtle, indeed fragile, manner: it has come to us quietly and directly, sewn into the center of her elegant quilt. Were it not for a family which has kept the oral history of the quilt alive, we might have missed Deborah Coates's message altogether. According to the family, two granddaughters of the maker could not agree on who should inherit the precious quilt, and so, with the Quaker sense of equality, it was decided to cut the quilt exactly in half. When the raw edges were bound over, the small central image was almost totally obscured. All that remained to be seen were a tiny foot on one quilt half and the edge of an arm on the other. Finally, the two halves came down together to a single descendant, along with the story of what lay within the seams. Recently, under the direction of a conservator, the bindings were opened and the fractured image was brought together for the photograph. In researching family history related to the quilt, a descendant has recently discovered that Lindley and Deborah Coates's home in Sadsbury, Lancaster County, Pennsylvania was Station #5 on one of the many routes of the Underground Railroad. This was clearly a family which found a variety of ways to express a strong moral commitment to justice and the emancipation of slaves.

Detail of Evening Star cradle quilt, 1836, Massachusetts, pieced cottons. Collection of the Society for the Preservation of New England Antiquities, Boston, Massachusetts.

and white women's groups, in 1833 and 1834. And already by 1834, drawing upon their experience of organized sewing for moral and reform purposes, women were holding fairs and bazaars at which they sold their needlework products to raise money for the abolitionist cause. From the 1830's until the eve of the Civil War, such fairs were a major source of funds for the abolitionist movement. Indeed, women's Anti-Slavery Societies outnumbered men's, and it was women who largely financed the abolitionist movement with their fund-raising activities—a crucial contribution that, together with their petition campaigns to Congress and their writings for abolitionist newspapers and magazines, has never, until recently, been taken seriously in any historical work.[95]

The first Anti-Slavery Fair was held in Boston in 1834, and it was so successful that the idea spread to other cities and towns throughout New England, and then to other states such as Ohio and Pennsylvania. The Boston Fair meanwhile became an annual and eagerly awaited event; and at its height it extended over ten days, from Christmas to New Year's. Regularly, too, detailed accounts of the Boston Fairs were carried in *The Liberator,* the abolitionist journal established in 1831 by William Lloyd Garrison.[96] The Fair advertised that it would sell "well made, useful, and ornamental products," and in 1838 the Salem, Massachusetts, Anti-Slavery Society underscored the "well made" by warning that "indifferent needlework" would be "suppressed"! Over the years, the Fairs displayed and sold every conceivable product of the needle. There were articles of apparel in abundance: shawls, scarves, caps, neckties, handkerchiefs, muffs, mitts and gloves, stockings, socks and baby shoes, gaiters and dressing gowns, knitted wool coats and embroidered capes, cuffs and collars; there were afghan blankets, tapestries ("of various styles...Historical, Floral, and Ornithological"), pin cushions and needlebooks, embroidered pictures and tablecloths, including one richly embellished with braid and embroidery made by the English activist and writer Harriet Martineau, which sold for one hundred dollars. And there were quilts: "cradle and bed quilts of Marseilles and American manufacture" in 1840; "a handsome quilt...looking as though the stitches were all measured from the first set" in 1853; and "patchwork comforters made in the best manner" in 1854. In 1846, *The Liberator* singled out for special comment a "North Star bed cover"—its name suggesting the star that guided slaves to freedom—made by a Lowell, Massachusetts, woman and described as "the most perfect and elegantly symmetrical thing of its kind." At first, the Fair organizers wanted only inscribed articles—textiles that would function as political texts—and the famous remark of Sarah Grimké, "May the point of our needles prick the slave owner's conscience," was regularly printed on needlebooks and, *The Liberator* noted, on the "handy work" that young children contributed to the cause. On some needlebooks, made in the form of shoes, was inscribed "Trample not on the oppressed." The Boston Anti-Slavery Fairs raised substantial amounts of money for the abolitionist cause, from six hundred dollars in the first year to $3700 in 1845 and five thousand dollars in 1854, for example; and the organizational and managerial skills demanded in running them provided women with a training they would put to use in yet another way with the outbreak of the Civil War itself.

Within days of Lincoln's first call for troops in April of 1861, northern women were organizing relief efforts, aware of the need to supplement the inadequate supplies of bedding and clothing available through the government and northern factories. Boston women, for example, organized delegations of needleworkers from all the city's churches, and with the help of the sewing machine produced five thousand shirts in five days.[97] Throughout the North, ten to fifteen thousand local Dorcas, Ladies Aid and Sewing Societies solicited money, donations of clothing and bedding and raw materials from local merchants from which they made additional clothing, blankets and quilts for the army.[98] (Even Lucy Larcom, despite her childhood aversion to patchwork, sewed bed quilts for the hospitals.)[99] By 1862, these relief efforts were organized, under the leadership of such remarkable women as Mary Livermore and others, as part of the work of the United States Sanitary Commission. A private organization designed to assist the War Department and the Medical Bureau in providing for the health and efficiency of the army, the Sanitary Commission concerned itself with the needs of the hastily established hospitals, recruiting nurses and providing food, bedding and medicines. As many

as seven thousand local women's aid societies were affiliated with the Sanitary Commission. They made and collected the supplies and shipped them to large central branches and storage depots, from whence they were systematically distributed to the hospitals. Bedding, including quilts, always desperately needed,

Lincoln predicted a six-week war when he called up the first recruits in April, 1861. No one could have foreseen the length or scope of the war, nor the horror and devastation which was to come. Women in both the North and South responded valiantly to the urgent call for help with relief efforts of various kinds. Northern women's volunteer aid societies supported the U.S. Sanitary Commission, serving the health and welfare of the troops. Women gathered vast amounts of needed supplies. Their efforts were so prodigious that one out of every six Union soldiers was warmed and comforted by a quilt that a mother, wife, sister or friend had made.

*Vintage photograph of a United States Sanitary Commission hospital, Civil War period.
Collection of the Library of Congress, Washington, D.C.*

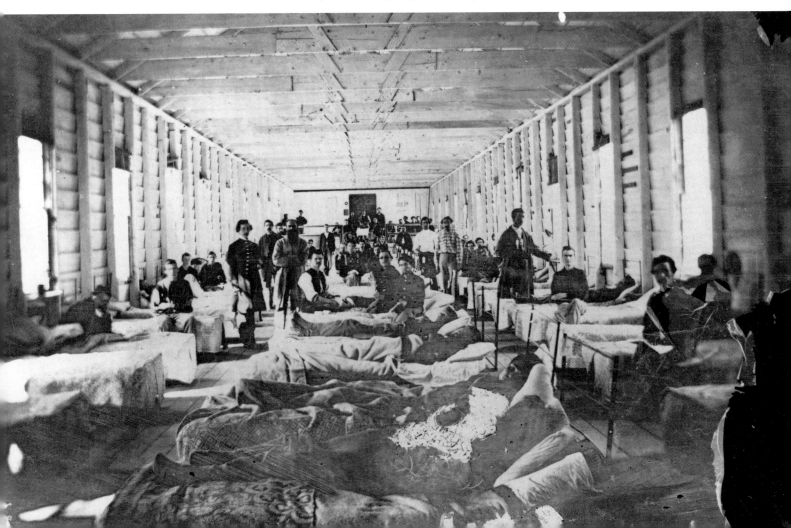

By 1863, small-town fund-raising efforts for hospital relief, which included local events like parties and picnics, had been consolidated into the concept of huge regional United States Sanitary Commission Fairs, lasting days and held in lavishly decorated halls. These fairs, conceived of and organized by women, were tremendously successful, and their importance did not go unnoticed. Abraham Lincoln said of women's efforts: "In this extraordinary war, extraordinary developments have manifested themselves, such as have not been seen in former wars; and amongst these manifestations nothing has been more remarkable than these fairs for the relief of suffering soldiers and their families. And the chief agents in these fairs are the women of America.... I have never studied the art of paying compliments to women; but I must say, that if all that has been said by orators and poets since the creation of the world in praise of women were applied to the women of America, it would not do them justice for their conduct during this war.... God bless the women of America." ‹Remarks at a Sanitary Fair in Washington made on March 18, 1864, as cited in The Life and Writings of Abraham Lincoln, ed. by Philip Van Doren Stern (New York: Modern Library, 1940), p. 805. ›

"Union Avenue, Great Central Sanitary Fair, June 1864."
Albumen print by Robert Newell in The Philadelphia Photographer,
October 1864. Courtesy of The Library Company of Philadelphia.

This rare photograph, found in an unpublished album of snapshots of the Allegheny fair of June 1–8, 1864, clearly attests to the importance of quilts in U.S. Sanitary Commission fair booths.

An 1864 photograph of a woman in a United States Sanitary
Commission fair booth, Allegheny, Pennsylvania. Collection
of The Carnegie Library of Pittsburgh, Pennsylvania.

This quilt was made by several women, but it was probably engineered and overseen by Cornelia Dow, a prominent woman of Portland, whose husband, Neal, was a major instigator of the first state-wide temperance law and a brigadier general in the Union army. At the time this quilt was completed, he had just been released from Libby Prison in Richmond, Virginia, in exchange for an imprisoned Confederate general.

A blatant statement about Union sympathies, this quilt's ink inscriptions range from the bloodthirsty to the witty and playful. The overall feeling is one of the utter righteousness and justness of the Union cause. The moral fervor seen here is made more interesting in light of the Dow family's passionate involvement in the temperance movement.

Detail of quilt below.

While our fingers guide the needle,

Our thoughts are in tente. (tents).

Friendship, 1864, Portland, Maine, 71 × 81 inches, pieced and appliquéd cottons, with ink work and embroidery. Collection of the Simmons family.

Medallion, by Elizabeth Keckley, probably Washington, D.C., c. 1860–1880, 86 × 81 inches, pieced, appliquéd and embroidered silks, with padding and fringe. Embellished with three-dimensional tassels. Collection of Ross Trump.

76

Elizabeth Keckley was born into slavery, her mother a slave and her father their master. Like her mother, Keckley became a specialized sewing slave and later used her considerable expertise as a seamstress to earn enough extra money to buy freedom for herself and her mulatto son. Later, Keckley employed the needle to further benevolent causes. In her autobiography, she talks about how she got the idea to adapt the concept of the Sanitary Commission fund raisers for her own cause, the Contraband Relief Association: "One fair summer evening I was walking the streets of Washington, accompanied by a friend, when a band of music was heard in the distance. . . . We quickened our steps, and discovered that it came from the house of Mrs. Farnham. The yard was brilliantly lighted, ladies and gentlemen were moving about, and the band was playing some of its sweetest airs. We approached the sentinel . . . and asked what was going on. He told us that it was a festival given for the benefit of the sick and wounded soldiers in the city. This suggested an idea to me. If the white people can give festivals to raise funds for the relief of suffering soldiers, why should not the well-to-do colored people go to work to do something for the benefit of the suffering blacks? I could not rest. . . . I made a suggestion in the colored church, that a society of colored people be formed to labor for the benefit of the unfortunate freedmen. . . . In two weeks 'the Contraband Relief Association' was organized, with forty working members." ‹Elizabeth Keckley, Behind the Scenes, Thirty Years a Slave and Four Years in the White House *(New York: Arno Press and* The New York Times, *1968), pp. 113–114.› Keckley organized the making and selling of needlework (among other things) at Contraband Relief Association fairs, and the organization eventually sent eighty boxes of goods to freedmen in Washington.*

Photographic portrait of Elizabeth Keckley, c. 1860–1870. Collection of Lloyd Ostendorf.

often led the list of wanted supplies, and it has been estimated that women supplied as many as 250,000 quilts and comforts, including both heirloom quilts donated from their homes and tied coverlets made specifically for the war effort.[100]

The culmination of their work came with the creation of the famous Sanitary Fairs that were held in major northern cities from 1863 through 1865. By 1863, Livermore recognized, "every city, town, and village had had its fair, festival, party, picnic, excursion, concert, and regular subscription fund" for hospital relief.[101] Indeed, Elizabeth Keckley, seeing such a Sanitary Commission fund-raiser in Washington, D.C., in 1862, was inspired to organize an analogous society, the Contraband Relief Association, for the benefit of the freed but suffering blacks.[102] Meanwhile, Livermore and Jane Hoge, who together with her headed the important northwestern district of the

Sanitary Commission (which included Wisconsin and parts of Illinois, Iowa, Michigan and Indiana), therefore conceived the idea of holding a massive fair at which needlework, art, antiques, books and other articles would be sold. The first great Fair, held in Chicago, was, Livermore recorded in her autobiography, "pre-eminently an enterprise of women, receiving no assistance from men in its early beginnings," and in fact "barely tolerated" by the male members of the Commission.[103] As the idea spread, the Fairs became massive events, extending over several days, held in halls lavishly decorated with banners, flags, trophies and floral displays and containing booths and exhibit spaces for the display of art, antiques and needlework, and featuring prizes, entertainment and refreshments. Fairs were held in Cincinnati, Cleveland, Philadelphia, New York and Boston as well as other major northern cities, and the amounts of money

Patriotic, by Mrs. Alfred Van Fleet, Illinois, 1866, 80 × 66 inches, pieced and appliquéd cottons, with embroidery.
Collection of the Yakima Valley Museum and Historical Association, Yakima, Washington.

*O*ne year after the end of the Civil War, Mrs. Alfred Van Fleet made this quilt, a unique personal record of that war and a tribute to her husband, a soldier who seems to have survived nearly fifty battles during 1862 and 1863. On the third white stripe from the top, Mrs. Van Fleet has embroidered her husband's name, military rank and affiliation, as well as a litany, arranged chronologically, of the forty-seven battles in Virginia, Pennsylvania and Maryland in which he fought. Why the list of Sergeant Van Fleet's battles ends in 1863 remains a mystery; we do know that he was shot off his horse at Gettysburg in 1863, but he survived and soon recovered to return to battle. He was not among the more than six hundred thousand men, North and South, who lost their lives in that cruel and bloody war.

raised were prodigious. The Philadelphia Fair in 1865 reported a profit of one million dollars; an eight-day fair in Iowa in 1864 raised fifty thousand dollars.[104] It is estimated that altogether the women's fairs raised four-and-a-half million dollars. When Henry Bellows, President of the Sanitary Commission, described the Chicago Fair as "a great national quilting party," he was paying an appropriate tribute to women whose needlework skills, and the organizational skills they had been developing for over a century in connection with the production and sale of that needlework, constitute an important chapter in their history and in that of the Civil War.[105]

Southern women, too, organized relief efforts for the war, providing, like their northern counterparts, essential clothing and bedding for the Confederate army. In the South, where factory production of textiles was still embryonic in 1861, and with the war shutting off the flow of manufactured goods from the North, the need for both clothing and bedding was even more acute. Lacking manufactured textiles, southern women found it necessary to revive, and

often to learn for the first time, pre-industrial handicraft processes in order to supply both military and their own civilian needs, including those of the slaves. "Manufactories have arisen where before the war they were not known," recorded one southern woman. "In every farm house the spinning-wheel and loom is heard." Mrs. Mary Jones, managing a large Georgia plantation, spent several months in 1862 seeking a flying shuttle for a hand loom and a carpet loom "such as the country people use for rag carpets at the North." By the end of that year, she had produced her first woven blanket and eighty yards of cloth. The cloth would then be used to create shirts and pants, quilts and comforts, for both soldiers and civilians. Unbleached muslin, and linsey, "the goods woven for Negro wear," were used for "all domestic purposes," including her own dresses, reported one white plantation woman.[106]

As in the North, women conducted their own relief efforts through their local Ladies Aid and Sewing Societies, and through others established for war relief. Soldiers Aid Societies and Ladies Clothing Asso-

Pillow, by Mary High Prince, Tennessee, 1910, 19 × 19 1/2 inches, pieced homespun cottons, with embroidery. Collection of Emeline P. Gist.

*M*ary Prince was barely into her twenties in 1861 when war came to Tennessee. Lives and property were not all that were destroyed in the next years. Fifty years later, the memory of the loss of a way of life suffered by southern white women was still strong enough to have moved Mary Prince to make a commemorative pillow, a truly remarkable memorial object. The poem she embroidered recalls the hardships southern women endured, in many cases having to learn or re-learn carding and spinning and the making of homespun. (Ironically, these women sometimes learned from slaves who, not having had access to manufactured goods, never forgot the primary processes.) The embroidered poem is surrounded by the homespun scraps of Civil War–period dresses, made and worn by Prince and her friends.

Women, Confederate and Yankee, found ingenious ways to support their causes. According to the Franklin County (Tenn.) Historical Review of January 1977, this quilt was "one of several made and raffled by the ladies of the Raus Community in Bedford County . . . during the Civil War as a means of raising money for the Confederacy." It was made by several women including Mary High, whose name appears on the quilt, as does that of Benjamin Prince, a soldier whom she would later marry. (Mrs. Prince made the pillow on page 79.) The couple were apparently very active and staunch supporters of the Confederacy; Prince was among a small band of rebels which never formally surrendered to the North.

Basket, by Mary High Prince and friends, Tennessee, 1863–1864, 96 × 74 inches, pieced and appliquéd cottons, with ink work. Collection of Emeline P. Gist.

ciations made and packed boxes of bedding and garments and produced prodigious quantities of flannel shirts and drawers, often by installing sewing machines in churches and working in groups. They held fairs at which they sold precious family treasures, including quilts, and they organized house-to-house campaigns for donations of linen tablecloths, napkins, sheets, and even "dimity counterpanes . . . and . . . the chintz furniture covers" to provide needed materials for bandages and compresses for the hospitals.[107] As in the North, the lack of adequate bedding was crucial, especially since many soldiers slept out of doors, and hospitals, often hastily erected in warehouses and other public buildings, were primitive at best. "We are sadly in want of comforts," wrote Kate Cumming from her post in a Confederate hospital, and black as well as white women made quilts. "A number of negro women are at work quilting comforts," she reported, noting that under the pressure of immediate need, the quilts were crudely constructed, of "unbleached homespun, and the raw cotton is put in them in lumps, and they are tacked about a foot apart." But, whether hastily or carefully made, they were appreciated, and Mrs. Mary Jones's daughter, working in a

hospital in Marietta, Georgia, wrote encouragingly to her mother in November of 1863 that the cots "all have nice sheets and comforts made of homespun. Some wards have calico comforts, and there is a piece of rag carpet spread by the side of every cot."[108]

Given the cost of textiles during the war, a calico comfort would indeed have been prized. Where calico was available at all, its price ranged from six to eight dollars a yard early in 1864 to twelve and sixteen dollars by the end of that year. You "take money to market in the market basket and bring home what you buy in your pocket-book," wryly observed Mary Chesnut, famous Civil War diarist. Aware of such cost and scarcity, Confederate soldiers retreating from Maryland would tuck into their knapsacks yards of calico, rolls of tape, spools of sewing thread and needlebooks (purchased perhaps at Anti-Slavery Fairs?) taken from the dead bodies of northern soldiers. In turn, northern troops raided southern homes, in one case carrying off, as an ex-slave remembered, "all de meat in de smokehouse, an' de blanket an' quilts an' every thing dey wanted." Thus, on both sides textiles were the support, and also the spoils, of war.[109]

Detail of quilt on page 80.

IN THE YEARS after the Civil War, as the nation began to recover from the divisions the war had created, women in the North and in the South joined in waging a different kind of war, a "crusade" as they called it, against alcoholism. The temperance movement was one of the largest of all nineteenth-century women's reform movements, sweeping across sections of the United States, in Frances Willard's words, "like wild prairie fire."[110] Despite its scope, it has been widely misunderstood. One must replace the commonly held picture of an axe-wielding Carrie Nation battering down the doors of saloons with that of a national movement, brilliantly organized, that worked skillfully and effectively for a variety of causes important to women's lives. From its founding in 1874 through the presidency of Willard from 1879 to 1898, the Woman's Christian Temperance Union not only addressed the issue of male alcoholism but also supported the eight-hour working day, child care for working women, vocational training for women, prison reform and suffrage. In time, the organization's work became international in scope, with unions in European and Asian countries, in North Africa, Australia and New Zealand, and its campaign in the 1880's and 1890's to curb not just liquor but drug traffic worldwide led to the creation of what became known as the Polyglot Petition—a mammoth scroll on which W.C.T.U. missionaries to foreign lands collected seven million names in fifty languages.[111] According to one contemporary historian, the W.C.T.U. became in the second half of the nineteenth century "the major vehicle through which women developed a changing role for themselves in American society."[112]

Beginning in the Northeast and the Midwest, the temperance movement spread to the South and included black as well as white women. Its members were primarily Protestant (and especially Methodist), middle and working class, many with previous experience in missionary work and in the Sanitary Commission. It was their church and home orientation that spurred them to invade male space—for they did dramatically enter the male preserve of the saloon, to

pray and persuade or, that failing, to disrupt business—and to undertake the related reform activities the organization sponsored. The sphere definition of women as custodians of morality that had encouraged many to enter into anti-slavery work was used by temperance women as well: the founder of the move-

*H*ere a towel, a most familiar and ordinary domestic object, is raised to the status of banner proclaiming a vehement and heartfelt political sentiment, victory over a very widespread domestic problem—alcoholism in the home.

Towel, c. 1900, possibly Illinois, 16½ × 36 inches, huck toweling, with crochet thread. Collection of Kathy Sullivan.

Vintage photograph of a Massachusetts W.C.T.U. meeting, c. 1880–1900.
Collection of the National Woman's Christian Temperance Union, Evanston, Illinois.

*T*he temperance movement began in the late eighteenth century. The curtailing of the sale of hard liquor was an issue throughout the nineteenth century, but women's participation burst into full flower with the Women's Temperance Crusade in Ohio in December 1873, when large groups of women marched together to saloons, entered and prayed, exhorting the owners to close down. These appeals were exceedingly successful. In Washington Court House, Ohio, eleven taverns closed within eight days, and eventually thousands of saloons closed their doors, if only for a short time. Nationwide, 750 breweries went out of business. In 1874, a superbly organized movement known as the Woman's Christian Temperance Union grew out of the crusade. A national organization based in the Midwest, it had a remarkably broad base: its hundreds of thousands of members were in every state and from every class. Attracting ordinary women under the banner of protecting the home from the ravages of alcoholism, it motivated its members to confront many other social problems. Frances Willard, the second president and the charismatic and visionary leader of the W.C.T.U., whose photograph is displayed prominently under the lectern, strategized brilliant campaigns for reform in a wide range of women's issues, among them child-labor laws, prison reform, support for rape victims, child-care centers and kindergartens, a shorter working day and the right to vote.

Drunkard's Path, c. 1875–1900, origin unknown, 74 × 77 inches, pieced cottons.
Collection of Bill and Maggie Pearson.

Back of the Crusade quilt, by Ohio W.C.T.U. members, 1876, 88 ½ × 98 inches, silks, with ink and stamp work. Collection of the National Woman's Christian Temperance Union, Evanston, Illinois.

*P*robibited from marking ballots, women made their opinions known by signing their names to pledges, petitions and quilts. Three thousand women used the pen to back their moral and political beliefs when they signed their names to the back of the Crusade quilt. It was made in 1876 to commemorate the famous Women's Temperance Crusade in Ohio in 1873, led by Eliza Jane Trimble Thompson. The quilt was made as a tribute to "Mother" Thompson and presented at the 1878 national W.C.T.U. convention in Baltimore. It was at this convention that Frances Willard made a speech in which she spoke of the political symbolism of quilts (see text, page 88). In her autobiography, Willard describes seeing this quilt at that convention: "The quilt contained a square of a different color for each State represented, and had, in embroidery, upon each square the device and motto of the several auxiliary organizations. It was a beautiful evidence of woman's skill and taste in needle handicraft, and as it hung in graceful folds from the gallery, was a banner (emphasis ours) of which no body of men or women need have been ashamed." ‹Frances E. Willard, Glimpses of Fifty Years (Chicago: H. J. Smith & Co., 1889), p. 77. ›

Feelings both for and against Frances Willard were intense. At the Chicago World's Columbian Exposition in 1893, Willard was honored as one of the four most respected and influential women of the nineteenth century. She was also vilified by some and placed in the company of the most despised elements of that century's culture—an idiot, a madman, an Indian and a criminal. The portrait of Willard chosen for this classic piece of propaganda is an especially formal one which implies a prudish, righteous and even fussy woman—an image many people hold of her today which belies her considerable warmth, humor and charisma.

American Woman and Her Political Peers, © 1893 by Henrietta Briggs-Wall. Sophia Smith Collection, Smith College, Northampton, Massachusetts.

ment, Mrs. E. T. Thompson of Hillsboro, Ohio, took her initial guidance from a verse she found in the Bible. In addition, the role of motherhood assumed special importance within the cult of domesticity, as we have seen. And it was both as mothers and as wives that women were threatened by male drinking. In the nineteenth century, alcohol was cheap and drinking was widespread; married women had only limited legal rights to their own property or to any wages they might earn; husbands might, and often did, drink up their own and their wives' assets. Vulnerable both to the sexual abuse of drunken husbands and to the economic destitution that threatened them and their children, many women saw in the temperance movement a way of establishing social controls that would give them more status and more actual power.

Under Willard's charismatic leadership, the W.C.T.U. developed tactics and strategies that brilliantly drew upon its members' domestic and moral allegiances.

The Union was described as one of "Organized Mother-Love"; "Home Protection" was its rallying cry, "For God and Home and Native Land" its motto. Meetings were conducted like church prayer meetings, and the rooms and halls where they were held were crowded with symbols: banners of silk, satin and velvet on the walls; great vases filled with grains, fruits and flowers; and speakers' platforms decorated to suggest, said Willard, "an interior as cozy and delightful as a parlor."[113] Above all, the women used both the organizational and the needlework skills of their church bazaars and charity fairs. Although herself keenly aware of the ambiguity of women's role in the churches, ironically commenting that their charity work was the one "department of church work where women have always been allowed an 'equal right' with men, viz.: that of paying off church debts and raising funds for 'church extension,'" Willard shrewdly encouraged and deployed these skills.[114]

Local women saw to it that there was a W.C.T.U. booth at every exposition, state or county fair, and the chapters employed quilts extensively as fund raisers, especially the ten-cent signature quilt that was so widely used by American women for a variety of fund-raising purposes throughout the century. Chapters made quilts and also embroidered hangings that displayed their chapter and state insignia. The genre of the friendship quilt was put to new use when, for example, Connecticut women created a quilt of silk *Shoo Fly* squares inscribed with the names of the members and officers of various chapters and presented it to their state president (page 15).[115] Quilts were made to celebrate the passage of state prohibition amendments; and of course innumerable quilts, still extant, made by individual women show their temperance sympathies through the use of the W.C.T.U.'s official colors of blue and white and through patterns such as *Drunkard's Path*.

The epitome of the association between textiles and temperance, however, came with the creation of what was called the Crusade quilt. Representing the contributions of over three thousand women whose signatures it bears, the quilt consists of variously colored silk and brocade squares on which are embroidered the devices and mottoes of W.C.T.U. state auxiliaries.

When the quilt was presented at the 1878 annual national W.C.T.U. convention in Baltimore, a speaker described it as symbolizing "women's patience in matters of detail—a quality that had been valuable in temperance reform." The advice literature, we may recall, had argued that patchwork taught just such

Ribbon, 1890, silk. Collection of the National Woman's Christian Temperance Union, Evanston, Illinois.

*S*ilk *ribbons, illustrated with photo-lithographs, are incorporated into many crazy quilts of the Victorian period. This ribbon illustrates an impressive thirteen-story building in Chicago which the National Woman's Christian Temperance Union built after they were asked to discontinue daily gospel temperance meetings at the local Y.M.C.A. building in 1883. In 1901, the Temple Trustees decided to honor the memory of Frances Willard by naming the structure Willard Hall and by paying off the $700,000 still owing on the building. The money came in fact from a fund-raising quilt and with penny donations from the many devoted W.C.T.U. members across the country. "In order to give all an opportunity to take part in this tribute, (the Trustees) have had a large number of Memorial boxes modelled with a fine cut of the Temple embossed on them, to be used in gathering in penny a day subscriptions. If during a year an average of 4,000 boxes could be filled in each state it would wipe out the entire debt on the building." ‹From an unpublished form letter to prospective financial supporters from the Temple Trustees, September 23, 1901, Chicago, in the collection of the National Woman's Christian Temperance Union, Evanston, Illinois. ›*

patience. Now, however, the rhetoric of the cult of domesticity was being used to justify women's active agency outside the home. Frances Willard also spoke, observing that "only a woman's convention would make so curious a testimonial." But she went further. The quilt, she said, deserved to be placed, as an example of protest, alongside the death sentence of a woman burned as a witch in Massachusetts, and the auction block on which a South Carolina woman slave had been sold. In thus associating the quilt with some of the most extreme examples of women's oppression, Willard significantly radicalized the meaning of quilts. As the Crusade quilt hung from the gallery in the convention hall where it was displayed, quilts had indeed moved off the beds to become banners, flags proudly carried by W.C.T.U. members in their moral and political "crusade." [116]

That Frances Willard should lead a movement that depended so heavily on the symbolism of quilts and of women's attachment to the home is indicative of the contradictions and complexities of women's lives that scholars of women's history are increasingly revealing. Like most of her constituency a product of small-town, midwestern Protestant America, raised

---

*W*ithin the span of a decade, Frances Willard, with the aid of her membership's missionary network in fifty countries, collected over seven million signatures on the Polyglot Petition. It called for the total international prohibition of alcohol and drug traffic and was displayed at Chicago's World's Columbian Exposition in 1893 and was later presented to President Cleveland and the Congress.

A vintage photograph of Frances Willard and Lady Somerset surrounded by the Polyglot Petition, c. 1895. Collection of Pat Ferrero.

*W*illard's political strategy of advocating women's rights in the name of protecting religion and the home converted many thousands of women who had previously been unmoved by female political activity. Quilts were widely used in the temperance movement as banners, petitions, fund-raising tools and symbols of that home. Willard, keenly aware of the political use of quilts, had herself hated sewing as a child. Yet in this photograph of her in her study, we can see that she apparently had a fondness for quilts: a crazy quilt adorns her sofa, and the entire study, with its wild collage of photographs of her many colleagues and friends, itself looks like such a quilt. The tireless Willard's personal motto was "Do Everything."

Vintage photograph of Frances Willard, working in her study, late nineteenth century. Collection of the National Woman's Christian Temperance Union, Evanston, Illinois.

Sampler, by Frances E. Willard, Janesville, Wisconsin, 1854, 8 × 10 inches, silk on linen. Collection of the National Woman's Christian Temperance Union, Evanston, Illinois.

*B*y the 1850's, the practice of young girls making samplers was waning. But, coming from strong New England ancestry, Frances Willard was required to make hers. The overriding character of Willard's sampler, which took her five years to make, is its ordinariness. It was something she had to do, and Frances made a minimal, competent, but uninspired job of it. She never liked sewing, and in her autobiography she talks about what her natural interests were: "It never occurred to me that I ought to 'know housework' and do it.... There was never a busier girl than I and what I did was mostly useful. I knew all the carpenter's tools and handled them: made carts and sleds, cross-guns and whip-handles, indeed, all the toys that were used at Fort House we children manufactured. But a needle and a dishcloth I could not abide—chiefly, perhaps, because I was bound to live out-of-doors." ‹ *Frances E. Willard,* Glimpses of Fifty Years *(Chicago: H. J. Smith & Co., 1889), p. 25.* ›

*F*rances Willard had close ties with her mother all through her life. In her years as the leader of the W.C.T.U., Willard lived with her secretary and long-time companion, Anna Gordon, and Mrs. Willard, who was an important part of Willard's network of organizations and activities. Mary T. H. Willard made this quilt as a gift to Frances on her fiftieth birthday, a fitting gift of respect and love from a Methodist woman. It is distinguished from many crazy quilts of the period by its sturdy wool fabrics and by its profusion of Biblical injunctions and wisdoms. In that same year, 1889, Frances Willard published her autobiography; the dedication reads: "Dedicatory. / THERE IS ONE 'Face that duly as the sun, Rose up for me since life begun;' ONE ROYAL HEART THAT NEVER FAILED ME YET. / TO MOTHER, AS A BIRTHDAY GIFT, ON JANUARY 3, 1889, THE EIGHTY-FIFTH ANNIVERSARY OF HER UNDAUNTED LIFE, I DEDICATE HER ELDEST DAUGHTER'S SELF-TOLD STORY."

Crazy, by Mary T. H. Willard, Illinois, 1889, 68 × 85 inches, embroidered wools. Collection of Sam and Nancy Starr.

by religious and industrious parents including a father who believed that domestic skills and a bit of music were all the education a daughter needed, Willard early rebelled against the domestic role. Her only finished piece of sewing was a sampler which took her five years and the forceful pressure of her mother to complete. "A needle and a dishcloth I could not abide," she wrote in her autobiography, and she much preferred making a Fourth of July flag to march with in a parade.[117] Yet she respected the importance of her members' domestic loyalties, addressing them, in the speeches for which she was famous, as her "beloved homemakers and housekeepers" who generously gave "scraps and fragments of their time" to the important work of reform.[118]

SUCH RHETORIC, so reminiscent of the advice literature of the cult of domesticity, would not characterize the woman's rights movement, ultimately the most far-reaching and important of all nineteenth-century women's reform efforts. For anti-slavery, Sanitary Commission and temperance women, needlework could justify and support political, relief and reform activity. A quilt—whether sent to a soldier, used as a fund raiser, or hung in a meeting hall—remained visible and tangible proof of women's continued commitment to their domestic role, even as it was being ingeniously used to expand that role, to help women claim more public and political space. For the woman's rights movement, however, sewing both utilitarian and ornamental was literal cause of women's inferior status: of their unpaid and undervalued work in the home and their exploited labor as factory textile workers and piece-workers. This new adversarial attitude towards women's sewing was voiced by leaders of the woman's rights movement such as Elizabeth Cady Stanton and Abigail Duniway. It was their response to the profound changes occurring in women's lives in the post–Civil War period, not the least of which was women's radically altered relationship to their traditional textile work. The increasing industrialization and urbanization of the United States in the post-war decades had led to more extreme disparities between urban and rural populations, to a class system that separated the rich and the poor, and therefore to a class stratification in women's sewing. The two extremes—underpaid and overworked textile workers on the one hand, and leisured women doing non-essential and time-consuming fancy needlework

on the other—came dramatically to epitomize women's subordinate status.

The plight of the textile worker had been a concern of the woman's rights movement from its inception. The Seneca Falls Convention that marked its official beginning in 1848 had included a series of reports on "how tradition and prejudice has kept [women] for the most part in one low-paid occupation, that of seamstress with wages ranging from thirty-one to thirty-eight cents a day."[119] And an early woman's rights publication, *The Una*, had carried articles describing the terrible conditions of the pieceworkers who sewed garments, especially men's shirts, in their rented rooms: long hours at low wages in badly ventilated and badly lighted attic spaces that led to tuberculosis, spinal curvature, blindness and starvation. By the end of the century, in an unbroken continuity from the time of the Lowell mills, women in the industrial labor force were still employed primarily in poorly paid textile work: in the clothing and garment trades, and in plants manufacturing cotton, silk, knit and other textile goods. Efforts to unionize them in order to improve wages and working conditions repeatedly failed, and such women remained therefore major examples of discriminatory wages and limited economic opportunity.[120]

At the other extreme were middle- and upper-class women, the wives and daughters of the new businessmen and entrepreneurs, who were being increasingly encouraged to engage in fancy needlework as symbol of their leisured status. The advice literature, including magazines like *Godey's,* had recommended that women do ornamental sewing, but only in moderation. Excessive fancy work was a misuse of a woman's time. Nevertheless, the vogue for needlework books such as Mrs. Pullan's, and the needlework columns and articles on sewing in *Godey's* itself, belied that counsel. *Godey's* provided needlework designs and instructions for everything from smoking jackets and lounging caps, antimacassars, tidies and doilies to ornamental dish ruffs and embroidered and appliquéd cashmere dog collars. Mrs. Pullan encouraged women to knit and net, learn point lace and crochet, braiding, embroidery and Berlin work, and "tatting or frivolité," all as ways of displaying their leisured status and their womanly natures.[121]

Stanton's attacks on sewing, according to one of her biographers, "caused considerable consternation, for sewing had become an accepted part of every woman's life." Her comments were often acerbic: as a

Crazy, c. 1880–1900, origin unknown, 70 × 70 inches, silks, velvets and taffetas, with embroidery and paint, and a lace border. Private collection.

It remains a mystery exactly what connection this quilt has with Sarah Josepha Buell Hale, the editor of Godey's Lady's Book *from 1836 to 1876. A like name ("S.J. Buell") is embroidered on the flag of the ship on the quilt, and the quilt itself is the epitome of the excesses which* Godey's *was extolling in decorative needlework towards the end of the century. Early in her life, Hale was widowed and found herself the sole support of her children. She was first a milliner and then went on to become one of the first women editors in America. In 1836, she was persuaded to work with* Godey's, *which was to become the most influential women's magazine of the day, reaching a staggering 150,000 subscribers by mid-century. Although by the end of the century* Godey's *was regarded as uncommonly fussy, in her own day Hale was a reformer who actively supported issues such as women's education, child welfare and dress reform. From 1833 to 1840, she founded and presided over the Seaman's Aid Society, which not only provided goods for destitute widows but had the then-radical vision of offering education and creating employment (sewing clothing for sailors) for these women.*

*Hexagon, by Abigail Scott Duniway, Oregon, pieced 1869, quilted 1900, 78 × 58 ½ inches, pieced silks and cottons.
Collection of the Oregon Historical Society, Portland.*

*A*bigail Duniway, living the life of an Oregon pioneer, also used the needle for survival. When her husband became an invalid, she became a milliner to support them and their six young children. Duniway despised sewing and also lacked a flair for it. Nonetheless, she succeeded in her business, and it was in her small shop that she heard the true stories of women's lives that propelled her to her next step. As soon as she could, she sold her millinery business to become the prolific and outspoken editor of The New Northwest, *a radical pro-suffrage weekly magazine which she founded in Portland. She had experienced political activism as a child: her parents were southern abolitionists before moving to the North.*

She apparently began this Hexagon quilt during the unhappy millinery period of her life, setting it aside when she picked up her pen. It is significant that she pulled it out again, many years later, to finish it. Handwritten on a silk piece attached to the border of the quilt: "This quilt was pieced in November 1869 by ABIGAIL SCOTT DUNIWAY of Oregon and was finished and quilted by her in November 1900 and donated to the first National Woman Suffrage Bazaar in honor of Theodore Roosevelt the first champion of the equal Suffrage movement ever elected to a National office by popular vote." She had planned to donate the quilt to the New York World's Fair in 1899 but, according to her biographer: "Immediately the other members of the Portland Woman's Club raised a special fund to purchase the quilt for the Oregon Historical Society. . . . Duniway used the money to aid the suffrage campaign of 1900." ❮Ruth Barnes Moynihan, Rebel For Rights, Abigail Scott Duniway *(New Haven: Yale University Press, 1983), p. 154.*❯

paid occupation, sewing was unhealthy and "the most miserable of trades"; as an amusement, it was "contemptible"; and "it should be the study of every woman to do as little of it as possible."[122] Women's fancy work, she charged, was simply a series of "digital absurdities." Her autobiography describes her visit to the niece of William Lloyd Garrison and her dismay at finding her busily embroidering a "cotton wash rag." Conversation, said Stanton, could not "rise above the wash rag level." Nor were the churches, through which so much of women's charity and reform sewing had been channeled, immune from her criticism. Stanton attacked a "pin-cushion ministry" that supported itself through its women members' needlework without in turn supporting their rights.[123] The suffrage activist Emily Collins, from a small town in western New York, agreed: "Would to Heaven that women could be persuaded to use the funds they acquire by their sewing-circles and fairs, in trying to raise their own condition...instead of spending the money in decorating their churches, or sustaining a clergy, the most of whom are trying to rivet the chains [of their subordination] still closer."[124]

In the early years of the woman's rights movement, sewing, and the institutions that supported it, such as quilting bees and sewing circles, functioned as they did for other reform groups, as a way both to raise funds and recruit new members. In the decades after 1848 and the Seneca Falls Convention, the tradition of holding bazaars, fairs and festivals to raise money did not disappear. Primarily, however, funds for the suffrage movement came from private cash donations, bequests in wills, membership dues in local chapters and the sale of tracts and other publications. The position of radical woman's rights advocates like Stanton, that the churches were a cause of woman's oppression, alienated large numbers of women until the issue was played down towards the end of the century, by which time the woman's rights movement had narrowed its focus to the single issue of getting the vote.

Quilts, meanwhile, as a major product of women's home sewing, also came under attack. For Abigail Duniway, Oregon pioneer and suffrage leader, they were, according to her biographer, an especial "bête noir." Every year Duniway reported in her newspaper, *The New Northwest,* on the Oregon State Fair, and she attacked the exhibits of hand needlework — "tatting, darned netting, silk embroidery," and "the ever obtruding and always ugly patchwork quilt." Quilts, she claimed, were "primary symbols of woman's unpaid subjection." In advancing this economic

Detail of quilt on page 95.

As women moved into the public sphere, into "the bigger family of the city and the state," fewer and fewer textiles were made which directly addressed women's issues. Quilts as the voice of disenfranchised women were no longer as necessary as they had once been. This quilt is a very rare (perhaps unique) exception and an important social document. It is an early quilt, made just a few years after the first United States National Women's Rights Convention in Seneca Falls, New York (1848). Its appliquéd vignettes visualize a woman engaged in activities considered very radical at the time: driving her own buggy with a banner advocating "WOMAN RIG{HTS}," dressed to go out while her husband wears an apron and, most surprising, speaking to a public meeting. How far women had come since 1837 when Angelina Grimké's speech to a public meeting was considered so shameful that it had caused a riot in Philadelphia! In 1849, Reverend James Fairchild wrote in his Woman's Rights and Duties (Oberlin, Ohio: James M. Fitch, 1849), p. 18: "It is a thing positively disagreeable to both sexes to see a woman a public character. With few exceptions, woman shrinks from it, and man can not but loathe it. Thus we are made."

interpretation, Duniway revealed the distance that she and others had traveled from earlier reformers, who valued quilts for their moral efficacy.[125]

Duniway's antipathy may also have been provoked by her discomfort with the Victorian culture that by the 1880's had firmly ensconced itself within Oregon's cities and towns, as it had throughout the rest of the nation. The fussy, crowded, over-decorated parlors of Victorian America typify that era for us today, and the silk, satin or velvet crazy quilt draped over a sofa, lounge or table is perhaps that parlor's most recognizable artifact. The emphasis on luxurious fabrics and decorative embroidery distinguishes crazy quilts from earlier patchwork, as does the use of commercial methods to promote them. Do-it-yourself kits containing pre-stamped fabric pieces and embroidery silks could be purchased, and the crazy quilt was widely advertised and promoted in print—a significant departure from the oral tradition in which earlier

quiltmaking was rooted. Frances Lichten has argued that the Victorian crazy quilts are "restless textiles," "protests against the shackles of needlework discipline."[126] As such, they suggest the breakdown of an earlier, more homogeneous quilt culture, and a shift in the meaning of quilts from earlier emphases on industry and moral virtue to those of conspicuous consumption and conspicuous display.

By the 1880's, the calico patchwork quilt had become associated with the past and with backward rural regions. Mrs. Pullan, we may recall, had spurned calico quilts as "valueless" as early as 1859. Fanny Bergen's 1894 article in *Scribner's* described quilts as products of "bygone times," no longer made except in "out of the way corners."[127] And the advice literature was by then arguing that it was no longer necessary to teach young children to do patchwork. Thus, the author of a book in 1874 on the education of young girls asserted that making patchwork would

*D*uniway, the leader of the woman's suffrage movement in the Northwest, worked for forty years to win women the right to vote. In 1914, six years before the franchise became national law, Duniway, at age 79, became the first woman to cast a ballot in the state of Oregon.

Vintage photograph of Abigail Scott Duniway casting her ballot, 1914.
Collection of the Oregon Historical Society (negative number OREG 4601), Portland.

96

simply lead to "fretfulness" in a small child whose muscles are "untrained" for the task and for whom physical exercise is more "salutary." And, in 1892, in the short story "Ann Lizy's Patchwork," New England author Mary Wilkins Freeman recognized the demise of the home training so long associated with learning to quilt. Ann Lizy resists doing her stint of four squares of patchwork before playing with a friend, and her grandmother finally surrenders to the new ways, telling her granddaughter to invite her friend over, "And tell her I said she'd better not bring her sewing . . . for you and she ain't goin' to sew any, and mebbe you'll like to go berryin', and play outdoors." [128] Freeman's story was indicative of the changing times, of the emergence of new attitudes on the part of women which would eventually lead some two million of them to support the suffrage movement by the time of the passage of the Nineteenth Amendment in 1920. [129]

By the end of the century, large numbers of women had entered the labor force, and not just as industrial textile workers. Improved educational opportunities, including access to college and post-graduate training, led to the emergence of a class of professional women—writers, teachers, and social workers in the new settlement house movement—many of whom chose professional careers over marriage. A new group of women white-collar workers was also developing, as expanding business and industry created an increasing need for secretaries, clerks, typists and telephone operators. Moreover, women's lives within the home were changing. A declining birth rate and new household technology—not only the sewing machine but gas heating, improved plumbing and municipal water supplies—gave middle-class wives a greater margin of free time, much of which they now spent not in church-related charity work or temperance work but in a new form of organization— women's clubs. These clubs, devoted to intellectual improvement and social reform, and in time organized into national federations, marked a significant departure from the more informal sewing circles and quilting bees of an earlier age. Women became less content to work indirectly for change through their sphere-attributed moral power, and they were in fact

rejecting the idea of separate spheres for women and men. Direct action via the vote was seen as essential to secure economic equality and political and legal rights. [130] The suffrage meetings and parades would flaunt flags and banners, but not the quilts that had so typified the Woman's Christian Temperance Union.

It was, however, historians agree, women's work in those earlier reform movements—abolition, the Sanitary Commission and the temperance movement— that provided them with the organizational experience and skills and that encouraged the sense of group solidarity and the development of political consciousness which were essential to the eventual success of the suffrage movement. If the suffragists repudiated women's sewing, they were nonetheless the inheritors of the rich reform experience which that sewing had so extensively sustained.

Today, as interest in quilts continues to grow, women are rediscovering in them values that the suffrage leaders, given their urgent need to focus attention on long overdue legal and economic reform, understandably chose to de-emphasize or ignore. As a quintessential product of women's sphere, quilts did represent the restricted role which woman's rights advocates correctly construed as insuring the continued inferior status of women. But, as scholars are now revealing, those "bonds of womanhood" that initially bound women to a restricted sphere also served to bind them together, and thus to generate that consciousness of themselves as a distinct group which enabled them, eventually, to enlarge their role and their lives. And quilts were an instrument in both that bonding and that emancipation. For many contemporary women therefore, aware of the potential and power of women as a group, and of the need for group definition and consciousness, the compelling fascination of quilts and quiltmaking resides in their enactment of just such processes of bonding: the joining into wholes of separate fragments of fabric, and the joining of women co-operatively engaged in creation and constructive change. As we look back over the extraordinary range of uses to which nineteenth-century women put their quilts—from ceremonializing a friendship or beautifying a home to wielding them as weapons in a sustained series of campaigns against social injustice—we can newly claim their quilt culture as a "heritage of our own." [131]

REFERENCE LIST

1. [Harriet Farley or Rebecca C. Thompson], "The Patchwork Quilt," *The Lowell Offering,* V (1845), as reprinted in Benita Eisler, ed., *The Lowell Offering: Writings of New England Mill Women (1840–1845)* (New York: Harper Colophon Books, 1977), p. 150; Eliza Calvert Hall, *"Aunt Jane" of Kentucky* (New York: A. L. Burt, 1907), p. 59.

2. See, for example, Susan Burrows Swan, *Plain & Fancy: American Women and Their Needlework, 1700–1850* (New York: Holt, Rinehart and Winston, 1977); Mirra Bank, *Anonymous Was a Woman* (New York: St. Martin's Press, 1979); C. Kurt Dewhurst, Betty MacDowell and Marsha MacDowell, *Artists in Aprons: Folk Art by American Women* (New York: E. P. Dutton, 1979); Linda Otto Lipsett, *Remember Me: Women & Their Friendship Quilts* (San Francisco: The Quilt Digest Press, 1985).

3. Emily Morrison Bondurant, *Reminiscences* [MS] (Chapel Hill: University of North Carolina Library, Southern Historical Collection), I, 74.

4. Edith White, "Memories of Pioneer Childhood and Youth...," in Christiane Fischer, ed., *Let Them Speak for Themselves: Women in the American West 1849–1900* (Hamden, Conn.: Archon, 1977), pp. 274–275; Clara Lenroot, *Long, Long Ago* (Appleton, Wisc.: Badger Printing Co., 1929), p. 7; Charlotte Perkins Gilman, *The Living of Charlotte Perkins Gilman* (New York: Harper & Row, 1975), p. 14.

5. Florence V. Kniseley Menninger, *Days of My Life: Memories of a Kansas Mother and Teacher* (New York: R. R. Smith, 1939), p. 28; Harriette Smith Kidder, *Diary* [MS] (New Brunswick, N.J.: Rutgers University Library), pp. 131–134.

6. Elmina Foster, *Papers* [MS] (Chapel Hill: University of North Carolina Library, Southern Historical Collection), p. 5; Caroline Cowles [Richards] Clarke, *Diary of Caroline Cowles Richards, 1852–1872* (Canandaigua, N.Y.: privately printed, 1908), p. 25; Helen Doyle, *A Child Went Forth: The Autobiography of Dr. Helen MacKnight Doyle* (New York: Gotham House, 1934), p. 45.

7. Caroline A. Stickney Creevey, *A Daughter of the Puritans* (New York: Putnam, 1916), p. 82; Ann Johnson, as told to Lenora Johnson MacDonald from 1912 to 1920, *Our Pioneer Mother* (privately printed, n.p., n.d.), p. 7.

8. Fannie Davis Veale Beck, *On the Texas Frontier* (St. Louis: Britt Printing and Publishing Co., 1937), p. 96; Mary B. King, *Looking Backward* (New York: Anson D. F. Randolph and Co., 1870), p. 16.

9. Lucy Larcom, *A New England Girlhood: Outlined from Memory* (Boston: Houghton Mifflin, 1889), pp. 122–123.

10. Mary A. Livermore, *The Story of My Life, or The Sunshine and Shadow of Seventy Years* (Hartford, Conn.: A. D. Worthington and Co., 1897), p. 87.

11. Larcom, *New England,* p. 122; King, p. 16; Margaret Isabella [Walter] Weber, *Reminiscences of Childhood* [MS] (Chapel Hill: University of North Carolina Library, Southern Historical Collection), p. 8.

12. Sandra Brant and Elissa Cullman, *Small Folk: A Celebration of Childhood in America* (New York: E. P. Dutton, 1981), p. 96.

13. Gerda Lerner, *The Grimké Sisters from South Carolina* (Boston: Houghton Mifflin, 1967), p. 17.

14. Bernice Carroll, *Liberating Women's History: Theoretical and Critical Essays* (Urbana: University of Illinois Press, 1976), p. 284.

15. For a fuller discussion of the cult, see "The Cult of True Womanhood," in Barbara Welter, *Dimity Convictions: The American Woman in the Nineteenth Century* (Athens: Ohio University Press, 1976).

16. Lydia Child, *The American Frugal Housewife,* 16th ed. (Boston: Carter, Hendee, 1835), p. 3. See also Lydia Sigourney, *Letters to Young Ladies* [1833] (London: Jackson and Walford, 1841); Eliza Leslie, *The Behavior Book* [1859] (New York: Arno, 1972).

17. Sarah Josepha Hale, *Manners; or Happy Homes and Good Society All the Year Round* (Boston: J. E. Tilton, 1868), p. 78.

18. Eliza Farrar, *The Young Lady's Friend* (Boston: American Stationer's Co., 1836), p. 122.

19. Farrar, p. 122; Sigourney, *Letters to Young Ladies* [1858], quoted in Welter, p. 33; Florence Hartley, *The Ladies' Handbook of Fancy and Ornamental Work,* [1859], quoted in Thomas K. Woodward and Blanche Greenstein, *Crib Quilts and Other Small Wonders* (New York: E. P. Dutton, 1981), p. 10.

20. Hale, p. 192. Cf. Mary P. Ryan's comment on the earlier training of young girls: "When a girl was trained for the economic specialities of the household, she was not necessarily socialized to femininity," *Womanhood in America from Colonial Times to the Present* (New York: Franklin Watts, 1975), p. 39.

21. For attitudes towards unmarried women see, for example, Shelly Zegart, "Old Maid, New Woman," *The Quilt Digest 4,* ed. Michael M. Kile (San Francisco: The Quilt Digest Press, 1986), pp. 54–65.

22. Nancy Cott, *The Bonds of Womanhood: "Woman's Sphere" in New England, 1780–1835* (New Haven: Yale University Press, 1977), p. 74.

23. In 1822, women were about sixty-five per cent of an estimated hundred thousand cotton-mill workers in the United States. Until 1850 they comprised two-thirds to three-fourths, and in some places nine-tenths, of all factory operatives. See Carl Degler, *At Odds: Women and the Family in America from the Revolution to the Present* (New York: Oxford University Press, 1980), p. 367; Thomas Woody, *A History of Women's Education in the United States* (New York: Science Press, 1929), II, 9.

24. For discussions of the experience of the New England mill girls, see Thomas Dublin, ed., *Farm to Factory: Women's Letters, 1830–1860* (New York: Columbia University Press, 1981); Hannah Josephson, *The Golden Threads: New England's Mill Girls and Magnates* (New York: Duell, Sloane & Pearce, 1949); Harriet Hanson Robinson, *Loom and Spindle: or Life Among the Early Mill Girls* (New York: T. Y. Crowell, 1898).

25. Catherine Clinton, *The Other Civil War: American Women in the Nineteenth Century* (New York: Hill & Wang, 1984), p. 28.

26. Larcom, *New England*, pp. 204, 255; Harriet Hanson Robinson, p. 81; Lerner, *The Grimké Sisters*, pp. 194, 275.

27. Quoted in Dublin, p. 13.

28. Larcom, *New England*, pp. 182, 193, 154.

29. "The Patchwork Quilt," as reprinted in Benita Eisler, pp. 150–154. This note of nostalgia survives in quilt circles today and can be credited, in part, with the popularity of the current revival of interest in quilts.

30. Dena S. Katzenberg, *Baltimore Album Quilts* (Baltimore: The Baltimore Museum of Art, 1982), pp. 61–62. The full story of the making of the Baltimore album quilts would also include the important role of Mrs. Achsah Goodwin Wilkins, whose protégée Mary Evans may have been, and who probably acted as mentor and supplier of fabric (her husband and her father-in-law owned a dry-goods store) to the "Ladies of Baltimore" quilt group who made many of the album quilts. Some of the album quilt block designs can be found on chintz coverlets designed by Mrs. Wilkins and executed under her supervision by black servants or slaves, skilled needlewomen whom she employed to do her sewing. See Katzenberg, pp. 63–65, and William Rush Dunton, Jr., *Old Quilts* (Catonsville, Md.: privately printed, 1946), pp. 187–188.

31. Leo Marx, *The Machine in the Garden* (New York: Oxford University Press, 1964), passim.

32. Katzenberg, pp. 34–36.

33. Letitia D. Miller, *Some Recollections of Letitia D. Miller* [MS] (Chapel Hill: University of North Carolina Library, Southern Historical Collection, 1926), p. 15; Elizabeth Buffum Chace, *Two Quaker Diaries,* with introduction by Malcolm R. Lovell (New York: Liveright, 1937), p. 45.

34. Sherbrooke Rogers, *Sarah Josepha Hale: A New England Pioneer, 1788–1879* (Grantham, N.H.: Tompson & Rutter, 1985), p. 121; Amelia Bloomer, *Life and Writings of Amelia Bloomer* (New York: Schocken Books, 1975), p. 168; Lloyd C. M. Hare, "An Island Girlhood One Hundred Years Ago," *The Dukes County Intelligencer,* V, 1 (August 1963), 11.

35. Kidder, p. 361; Ann Johnson, p. 27; Elizabeth Welty, *Letters* [MS] (Columbia: University of Missouri Library, Joint Collection, University of Missouri, Western Historical Manuscript Collection, State Historical Society of Missouri).

36. Eliza Ann (Marsh) Robertson, *Papers, 1849–1872* [MS] (Chapel Hill: University of North Carolina Library, Southern Historical Collection), letter of March 24, 1856.

37. Rogers, p. 121; Deborah S. Gardner, " 'A Paradise of Fashion': A. T. Stewart's Department Store, 1862–1875," in Joan M. Jensen and Sue Davidson, *A Needle, a Bobbin, a Strike* (Philadelphia: Temple University Press, 1984), p. 71.

38. Ruth E. Finley, *The Lady of "Godey's": Sarah Josepha Hale* (Philadelphia: J. P. Lippincott, 1931), p. 156. On manufactured men's clothing see Elizabeth Faulkner Baker, *Technology and Women's Work* (New York: Columbia University Press, 1964), pp. 24–25.

39. Mrs. (Matilda Marian [Chesney]) Pullan, *The Lady's Manual of Fancy Work: A Complete Instructor in Every Variety of Ornamental Handiwork* (New York: Dick and Fitzgerald, 1859), pp. xiv–xv.

40. Pullan, p. 95.

41. Jonathan Holstein in Ruth Andrews, ed., *How to Know American Folk Art* (New York: E. P. Dutton, 1977), p. 129.

42. On improved fiber quality, see Victor S. Clark, *History of Manufactures in the United States* (New York: McGraw-Hill, 1929), II, 386–391; on colors available, Mary Barton, unpublished talk at Show-Me Quilt Symposium, July 31 to August 2, 1980, Columbia, Missouri; on thread manufacture, Rachel Maines, "American Needlework in Transition, 1880–1930," in *Papers in Women's Studies* (Ann Arbor, Mich.: Women's Studies Program, 1978), pp. 57–84. See also Jonathan Holstein, "The American Block Quilt," in Jeannette Lasansky, ed., *In the Heart of Pennsylvania: Symposium Papers* (Lewisburg, Penn.: Oral Traditions Project, 1986), pp. 16–26; Rachel Maines, "Paradigms of Scarcity and Abundance/The Quilt as an Artifact of the Industrial Revolution," in Lasansky, pp. 84–89; and Holstein in Andrews, p. 129.

43. Eleanor Flexner, *Century of Struggle: The Woman's Rights Movement in the United States* (New York: Atheneum, 1968), p. 78; Charles A. Beard and Mary R. Beard, *The Rise of American Civilization* (New York: Macmillan, 1930), pp. 653–660.

44. Lucy Larcom, "Weaving," as reprinted in Elaine Hedges and Ingrid Wendt, eds., *In Her Own Image: Women Working in the Arts* (New York: The Feminist Press/McGraw-Hill, 1980), pp. 39–41.

45. Letitia Burwell, *A Girl's Life in Virginia Before the War* (New York: F. A. Stokes, [c. 1895]), p. 194.

46. Catherine Clinton, *The Plantation Mistress: Woman's World in the Old South* (New York: Pantheon Books, 1982), p. 26.

47. Sarah Frances (Hicks) Williams, *Papers, 1838–68* [MS] (Chapel Hill: University of North Carolina Library, Southern Historical Collection), letters of February 3, 1855, and December 10, 1853.

48. George P. Rawick, ed., *The American Slave: A Composite Autobiography* (Westport, Conn.: Greenwood, 1972), III, part 4, p. 126.

49. Williams, letter of January 16, 1858. Comparable prices at the time were twelve hundred dollars for an adult male, one thousand dollars for a thirteen-year-old boy.

50. Eugene D. Genovese, *Roll Jordan Roll: The World the Slaves Made* (New York: Pantheon Books, 1974), pp. 7, 495.

51. See footnote 48. Rawick's publication comprises nineteen volumes of interviews, upon which I have drawn in the following discussion.

52. Norman R. Yetman, ed., *Voices from Slavery* (New York: Holt, Rinehart & Winston, 1970), p. 227. Also in Rawick, XV, part 1, pp. 129-130.

53. William Loren Katz, ed., *Five Slave Narratives* (New York: Arno, 1969), pp. 18-19; Genovese, p. 529.

54. Rawick, V, part 2, p. 124; XVI, p. 14; V, part 1, p. 55; IV, part 2, p. 18.

55. Rawick, XIII, part 1, p. 81.

56. Elizabeth Keckley, *Behind the Scenes, or, Thirty Years a Slave, and Four Years in the White House* (New York: G. W. Carleton & Co., 1868), pp. 45, 49, 55.

57. Rawick, III, part 3, p. 180; Genovese, p. 557; Rawick, XII, part 1, p. 307.

58. Rawick, IV, part 2, pp. 1, 51. On dyeing with red clay, see Karoline Patterson Bresenhan and Nancy O'Bryant Puentes, *Lone Stars: A Legacy of Texas Quilts, 1836-1936* (Austin: University of Texas Press, 1986), p. 42. Red clay dyeing was popular for many generations before and after the Civil War in southern states with red clay deposits.

59. For information on slave quiltings see Rawick, IV, part 1, p. 261; V, part 2, p. 136; VII, p. 62; and Charles L. Perdue, Jr., Thomas E. Barden and Robert K. Phillips, *Weevils in the Wheat: Interviews with Virginia Ex-Slaves* (Charlottesville: University of Virginia Press, 1976), p. 252.

60. Rawick, I (*From Sundown to Sunup*), pp. 55, 32.

61. Important researchers of antebellum black quilts are Cuesta Benberry, St. Louis, Missouri; Gladys Marie Fry, University of Maryland, College Park; and Maude Wahlman, University of Central Florida, Orlando.

62. Alice Walker, "In Search of Our Mothers' Gardens," *Radcliffe Quarterly,* June 1974, pp. 5, 6; reprinted in Walker, *In Search of Our Mothers' Gardens* (San Diego: Harcourt Brace Jovanovich, 1983).

63. Keturah Belknap, "Keturah Penton Belknap Journals," in Cathy Luchetti, *Women of the West* (St. George, Utah: Antelope Island Press, 1982), pp. 140-141; on Belknap, see also Glenda Riley, *Frontierswomen: The Iowa Experience* (Ames: University of Iowa Press, 1981), pp. 15-16; Mary E. Hampton, quoted in Annie Doom Pickrell, *Pioneer Women in Texas* (Austin: The Pemberton Press, 1970), p. 133; Sue Sanders, *Our Common Herd* (New York: Garden City, 1939), p. 72.

64. Miriam Davis Colt, diary entry of March 15, 1856, quoted in Jens Christian Bay, *A Heroine of the Frontier* (Cedar Rapids, Iowa: privately printed, 1941).

65. Lillian Schlissel, *Women's Diaries of the Westward Journey* (New York: Schocken Books, 1982), p. 14. Cf. John Mack Farragher, *Women and Men on the Overland Trail* (New Haven: Yale University Press, 1979).

66. See, for example, Lipsett, passim.

67. Sarah J. Walden Cummins, *Autobiography and Reminiscences* (LaGrande, Ore.: LaGrande Publishing Co., 1914), p. 54.

68. Catalogue files, Textile Division, Nebraska Historical Society, Lincoln; the blue-and-white Vermont quilt is now in the Minnesota Historical Society collection, St. Paul.

69. Virginia Wilcox Ivins, *Pen Pictures of Early Western Days* (Keokuk, Iowa: [n.p.], 1908), p. 64.

70. Schlissel, p. 58.

71. Quoted from the 1849 diary of Catherine Haun in Schlissel, p. 183; see also Abigail Duniway, *Captain Gray's Company: or, Crossing the Plains and Living in Oregon* (Portland, Ore.: S. J. McCormick, 1859), p. 107.

72. Rosalynn Baxandall, Linda Gordon and Susan Reverby, *America's Working Women: A Documentary History, 1600 to the Present* (New York: Random House, 1976), pp. 70, 71; Luchetti, p. 80; Riley, p. 16.

73. Joyce Gross, *A Patch in Time* (Mill Valley, Calif.: Mill Valley Quilt Authority Show, 1973), p. 31.

74. Mrs. Lois Hagen, *Parish in the Pines* (Caldwell, Idaho: Caxton Printers, 1938), p. 32.

75. Henrietta C. Jones, *Sketches from Real Life* (Watertown, N.Y.: n.p., 1898), p. 100; Luna Kellie, *Memoirs of Luna Kellie* [MS] (Lincoln: Nebraska Historical Society), p. 17; Lucy Larcom, *Life, Letters, and Diary,* ed. Daniel Dulaney Addison (Detroit: Gale Research Co., 1970), p. 29.

76. Barbara Brackman, "Charlotte Jane Whitehill—Appliqué Artist," *Quilter's Newsletter Magazine,* April 1980, p. 23; Grace Snyder, *No Time on My Hands,* as told to Nellie Snyder Yost (Caldwell, Idaho: Caxton Printers, 1963), p. 15.

77. L. A. Nash, "Sunny Ranche Chapters," *The Woman's Magazine,* August 1889, p. 361.

78. Schlissel, p. 74, n. 23; Kellie, pp. 4, 13; Rebecca Hildreth Nutting Woodson, *A Sketch of the Life of Rebecca Hildreth Nutting (Woodson) and Her Family* [MS] (Berkeley: The University of California, Bancroft Library); Mrs. Gertrude van Rensselaer Wickham, ed., *Memorial to the Pioneer Women of the Western Reserve* (Cleveland: Women's Department of the Cleveland Centennial Commission, 1896), p. 22; Mrs. Robert Henry, quoted in Pickrell, p. 167.

79. Patricia Mainardi, "Quilts: The Great American Art," *The Feminist Art Journal,* Winter 1973, p. 20; Mrs. Elsie Dubach Isely, *Sunbonnet Days* (Caldwell, Idaho: Caxton Printers, 1935), pp.

78–79; Sara T. L. Robinson, *Kansas: Its Interior and Exterior Life,* 7th ed. (Boston: Crosby, Nichols and Co., 1857), pp. 215–216; Zona Gale, *Friendship Village* (New York: Macmillan, 1908), p. 113.

80. Rolla Tryon, *Household Manufactures in the United States, 1640–1860* (Chicago: University of Chicago Press, 1917), p. 184.

81. Katherine Krebs, *Back Home in Pennsylvania* (Philadelphia: Dorrance and Co., 1937), p. 43; [Mary Haines Harker], "Journal of a Quaker Maid," *Virginia Quarterly Review,* XI (1935), 81.

82. "Susan McCord's Legacy," in Robert Bishop, *New Discoveries in American Quilts* (New York: E. P. Dutton, 1975), pp. 111–114.

83. See, for example, Annette Kolodny, *The Land Before Her: Fantasy and Experience of the American Frontier, 1630–1860* (Chapel Hill: University of North Carolina Press, 1984); Suellen Meyer, "Pine Tree Quilts," *The Quilt Digest 4,* pp. 6–19.

84. Joyce Parr, "Effects of Isolation on the Woman Artist," in Beth Reed, ed., *Toward a Feminist Transformation of the Academy: Proceedings of the Fifth Annual GLCA Women's Studies Conference* (Ann Arbor, Mich.: The Great Lakes College Association, Women's Studies Program, 1980), pp. 31–33.

85. Mary P. Ryan, *Cradle of the Middle Class: The Family in Oneida County, New York, 1790–1865* (Cambridge, England: Cambridge University Press, 1981), p. 54.

86. Degler, p. 300; Keith E. Melder, "Ladies Bountiful: Organized Women's Benevolence in Early Nineteenth-Century America," *New York History,* XLVIII (1967), 237; Ryan, *Cradle,* p. 215.

87. Kidder, entry for November 12, 1846.

88. Louisa A. Nash, "The Women Workers of the Episcopal Church," in Mary O. Douthit, ed., *The Souvenir of Western Women* (Portland, Ore.: Presses of Anderson & Duniway Co., 1905), p. 99.

89. Jones, p. 212.

90. Frances Trollope, *Domestic Manners of the Americans* (New York: Dodd, Mead and Co., 1901), II, 14; Helen Clark, "What Christianity Has Done for the Indian Woman," in Douthit, p. 164.

91. Doyle, p. 162.

92. Rayna Green, ed., *That's What She Said: Contemporary Poetry and Fiction by Native American Women* (Bloomington: Indiana University Press, 1984), p. 315.

93. See Elizabeth Akana, "Ku'u Hae Aloha," *The Quilt Digest 2* (San Francisco: Kiracofe and Kile, 1984), pp. 70–77.

94. Carrie A. Hall and Rose G. Kretsinger, *The Romance of the Patchwork Quilt in America* (Caldwell, Idaho: Caxton Printers, 1935), p. 65.

95. Gerda Lerner, "Placing Women in History: A 1975 Perspective," in Carroll, pp. 361–362. According to more recent research, a black Female Antislavery Society was formed in Salem, Massachusetts, in 1832. See the unpublished diss. (University of California, Irvine, 1982) by Willie Mae Coleman, "Keeping the Faith and Disturbing the Peace. Black Women: From Anti-Slavery to Women's Suffrage," p. 14.

96. All subsequent references to the Boston Anti-Slavery Fairs are taken from the annual reports in *The Liberator,* January 1834 to December 1865 (American Periodical Series, microfilm, reels 391–399).

97. Mary A. Livermore, *My Story of the War: A Woman's Narrative of Four Years Personal Experience as a Nurse in the Union Army* (New York: Arno, 1972), p. 111.

98. Virginia Gunn, "Quilts for Union Soldiers in the Civil War," in *Uncoverings 1985,* ed. Sally Garoutte (Mill Valley, Calif.: American Quilt Study Group, 1986), pp. 95–121.

99. Larcom, *Life,* p. 109.

100. Gunn, p. 114.

101. Livermore, *My Story,* p. 409.

102. Keckley, pp. 113–114.

103. Livermore, *My Story,* p. 413.

104. Livermore, *My Story,* passim; Edward T. James, ed., *Notable American Women, 1607–1950: A Biographical Dictionary* (Cambridge, Mass.: Harvard University Press, 1971), II, 410–413; Gunn, passim; Riley, p. 134.

105. Gunn, p. 115.

106. Kate Cumming, *Kate: The Journal of a Confederate Nurse,* ed. Richard Barksdale Harwell (Baton Rouge: Louisiana State University Press, 1959), p. 82; Robert Manson Myers, ed., *The Children of Pride: A True Story of Georgia and the Civil War* (New Haven: Yale University Press, 1972), pp. 949, 984; Letitia D. Miller, p. 13.

107. Emma Holmes, *The Diary of Emma Holmes,* ed. John F. Marszaler (Baton Rouge: Louisiana State University Press, 1979), p. 77; Mrs. Roger A. Pryor, *Reminiscences of Peace and War,* as excerpted in Mary Beard, ed., *America Through Women's Eyes* (New York: Greenwood Press, 1976), p. 207.

108. Cumming, p. 188; Myers, p. 1117.

109. Myers, pp. 1134, 1211; Mary Boykin Chesnut, *A Diary from Dixie,* ed. Isabella D. Martin and Myrta Lockett Avary (New York: Peter Smith, 1929), p. 284; Constance Cary Harrison, *Recollections Grave and Gay* (New York: Charles Scribner's Sons, 1911), p. 135; Rawick, VII, part 2, p. 70.

110. Frances E. Willard, *Women and Temperance or the Work and Workers of the Woman's Christian Temperance Union* (Hartford, Conn.: Park Publishing Co., 1883), p. 78.

111. Mary Earhart, *Frances Willard: From Prayers to Politics* (Chicago: University of Chicago, 1944), pp. 340–343.

112. Ruth Bordin, *Women and Temperance: The Quest for Power and Liberty, 1873–1900* (Philadelphia: Temple University Press, 1981), p. xviii.

113. Frances E. Willard, *Glimpses of Fifty Years: The Autobiography of an American Woman* (Chicago: H. J. Smith and Co., 1889), pp. 330, 471.

114. Willard, *Women,* p. 114.

115. Typescript describing Connecticut State W.C.T.U. Convention of 1887, Archives, W.C.T.U. Headquarters, Evanston, Illinois. Courtesy of Pat Ferrero.

116. Willard, *Women,* pp. 77–79.

117. Willard, *Glimpses,* p. 25.

118. Quoted in Sheila M. Rothman, *Woman's Proper Place: A History of Changing Ideas and Practices, 1870 to the Present* (New York: Basic Books, 1978), p. 67.

119. Alma Lutz, *Created Equal: A Biography of Elizabeth Cady Stanton* (New York: John Day, 1940), p. 51.

120. Caroline Healy Dall and Paulina Wright Davis, eds., *The Una* (Providence, R.I.), I (1853), II (1854), passim; Flexner, p. 230.

121. Arlene Zeger Wiczyk, *A Treasury of Needlework Projects from "Godey's Lady's Book"* (New York: Arco, 1972), passim; Mrs. (Eliza) Warren and Mrs. Pullan, *Treasures in Needlework* [1870] (New York: Lancer Books, 1973), passim.

122. Lutz, p. 58.

123. Elizabeth Cady Stanton, *Eighty Years and More (1815–1897): Reminiscences of Elizabeth Cady Stanton* (New York: European Publishing Co., 1898), p. 435; Elizabeth Cady Stanton, *History of Woman Suffrage* (New York: Arno, 1969), p. 851.

124. Emily Collins, *Reminiscences of Emily Collins,* as excerpted in Alice Rossi, ed., *The Feminist Papers: From Adams to de Beauvoir* (New York: Columbia University Press, 1973), p. 423.

125. Ruth Barnes Moynihan, *Rebel for Rights, Abigail Scott Duniway* (New Haven: Yale University Press, 1983), p. 153.

126. Penny McMorris, *Crazy Quilts* (New York: E. P. Dutton, 1984), pp. 9, 16–17; Frances Lichten, *Decorative Arts of the Victorian Era* (New York: Charles Scribner's Sons, 1950), p. 178.

127. Fanny D. Bergen, "The Tapestry of the New World," *Scribner's,* XXI, 3 (September 1894), 360.

128. Anna Callender Brackett, *The Education of American Girls* (New York: Putnam's, 1874), p. 20; Mary Wilkins Freeman, "Ann Lizy's Patchwork," *Young Lucretia and Other Stories* (Freeport, N.Y.: Books for Libraries Press, 1970), p. 84.

129. Ryan, *Womanhood,* p. 231.

130. On the changes in women's lives, see Flexner, pp. 179–180, and Margaret Gibbons Wilson, *The American Woman in Transition: The Urban Influence 1870–1920* (New York: Greenwood Press, 1979).

131. The phrase is taken from Nancy F. Cott and Elizabeth H. Pleck, eds., *A Heritage of Her Own: Toward a New Social History of American Women* (New York: Simon & Schuster, 1979). The double meaning of the "bonds of womanhood" is especially explored by Cott in *The Bonds of Womanhood,* cited in footnote 22.

*T*he Quilt Digest series. Collect each volume in this annual series which highlights exceptional antique and contemporary quilts and the writings of the world's foremost quilt experts. By doing so, you will assemble an up-to-date, authoritative encyclopedia of quilt information and photographs. There is nothing like *The Quilt Digest.*

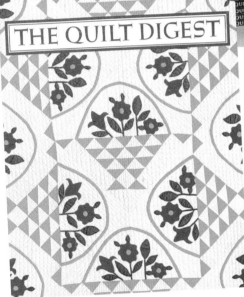

Other Books from...

◄*The Quilt Digest 5.* Extraordinary quilts from around the world, plus a portrait of six international quiltmakers, an exploration of how quilts unite the generations, unusual antique quilts made from fabrics issued by tobacco companies, the first comprehensive presentation of antique Australian quilts, a look at a trailblazing collection of antique and contemporary quilts. 80 pages. 78 color photographs. $16.95.

1. *The Quilt Digest 1.* Remarkable quilts, plus Michael James interview, *Log Cabin* quilts, Amish home interiors, a Jewish immigrant's quilt, the Esprit Amish collection, quilt documentation techniques. 72 pages. 52 color and 18 black-and-white photographs. $14.95.

2. *The Quilt Digest 2.* Many rare quilts, plus a superb private collection, vintage photos of crazy quilts in a Victorian home, a pioneer wife and her quilt, quilt care and conservation, Hawaiian Flag quilts. 80 pages. 60 color photographs and 17 black-and-white photographs and illustrations. $14.95.

3. *The Quilt Digest 3.* Dozens of exceptional quilts, plus Quaker quilts, formal Southern quilts from the Charleston (South Carolina) Museum collection, a short story about a wife and husband and their quilt, eccentric quilts, an Alabama pioneer and her quilts. 88 pages. 93 color photographs. $15.95.

4. *The Quilt Digest 4.* A variety of exceptional quilts, plus *Pine Tree* quilts, a black, self-help quilting co-operative, a nineteenth-century "old maid" and the quilt made for her by her quilting-bee friends, quilts in modern art, a quilt dealer's private collection. 88 pages. 75 color and 8 black-and-white photographs. $16.95.

5. *The Adventures of Sunbonnet Sue.* Internationally known quiltmaker Jean Ray Laury has plucked familiar Sunbonnet Sue off the tranquil surface of her quilt and plunged her into the turbulent everyday life of a harried wife and mother. As a quilt enthusiast, you will appreciate Sue's awe-inspiring adventures: you may even recognize many of them as your own as you giggle, then guffaw your way through this hilarious cartoon series. All drawings by the author. 24 pages each. $4.95 each.

6. *Homage to Amanda* by Edwin Binney, 3rd and Gail Binney-Winslow. A great quilt collection bountifully illustrates this concise guide to the first two hundred years of American quiltmaking. Published by Roderick Kiracofe/R K Press and distributed exclusively by The Quilt Digest Press. 96 pages. 71 color photographs. $18.95.

THE QUILT DIGEST PRESS

Hearts and Hands: The Influence of Women & Quilts on American Society by Pat Ferrero, Elaine Hedges and Julie Silber. Within the stunning, photograph-laden pages of this book is revealed the important role played by women and quilts in the last century's great movements and events—industrialization, the abolition of slavery, the Civil War, the westward expansion and pioneer experience, temperance and suffrage. Once you have read this extraordinary book, you will never forget it. 112 pages. 53 color and 39 black-and-white photographs. $19.95 paperback. $29.95 hard cover. ▼

7. The Art Quilt by Penny McMorris and Michael Kile. Quilts made by sixteen leading quiltmakers especially for this landmark book are the focus of a fascinating, in-depth look at this century's quiltmaking movement and the emergence of the contemporary quilt. A remarkable achievement. 136 pages. 79 color and 8 black-and-white photographs. $21.95 paperback. $29.95 hard cover. $10.00 fine-art poster.

8. Remember Me: Women & Their Friendship Quilts by Linda Otto Lipsett. A thorough examination of friendship quilts and an intimate portrait of seven nineteenth-century quiltmakers who made them, rendered in astonishing detail. A uniquely personal book that will transport you back into an earlier time. 136 pages. 112 color and 23 black-and-white photographs. $19.95 paperback. $29.95 hard cover.

Ordering Information. Thousands of quilt, antique, book and museum shops around the world carry the books and posters we publish. Check with shops in your area. Or you may order directly from us.

To order, send us your name, address, city, state and zip code. Tell us which books or posters you wish to order and in what quantity. California residents add 6½% sales tax. Finally, to the price of the books or posters you order, add $1.75 for the first book or poster—or any number of Sunbonnet Sue books—and $1.00 for each additional book or poster to cover postage and handling charges. Enclose your check made payable to *The Quilt Digest Press* and mail it, along with the above information, to Dept. D, 955 Fourteenth Street, San Francisco 94114.

Readers outside North America may have their orders shipped via air mail by including $8.00 for each book or poster—or Sunbonnet Sue set—ordered. All orders must be accompanied by payment in U.S. dollars drawn on a U.S. bank.

Depending upon the season of the year, allow 4–6 weeks for delivery. Readers outside North America should allow several additional weeks for sea delivery.

We are happy to send gift books or posters directly to recipients.

Wholesale information is available to retailers upon request.

Our Mailing List. If your name is not on our mailing list and you would like it to be, please write to us. We will be happy to add your name so that you will receive advance information about our forthcoming books.